A BULL
IN CHINA

ALSO BY JIM ROGERS

Hot Commodities:
How Anyone Can Invest Profitably
in the World's Best Market

Adventure Capitalist:
The Ultimate Road Trip

Investment Biker:
Around the World with Jim Rogers

A BULL
IN CHINA

★ ★ ★ ★ ★

INVESTING PROFITABLY
IN THE WORLD'S
GREATEST MARKET

JIM ROGERS

BICENTENNIAL
BICENTENNIAL
1807
WILEY
2007
BICENTENNIAL
BICENTENNIAL

John Wiley & Sons, Ltd

Published in the UK in 2007 by   John Wiley & Sons Ltd,
                                     The Atrium, Southern Gate, Chichester,
                                     West Sussex PO19 8SQ, England
                                     Telephone   (+44) 1243 779777

Email (for orders and customer service enquiries): cs-books@wiley.co.uk
Visit our Home Page on www.wiley.com

First published in the United States by Random House. This edition published by arrangement with Random House, an imprint of The Random House Publishing Group, an imprint of Random House, Inc.

Other Wiley Editorial Offices

John Wiley & Sons Inc., 111 River Street, Hoboken, NJ 07030, USA

Jossey-Bass, 989 Market Street, San Francisco, CA 94103-1741, USA

Wiley-VCH Verlag GmbH, Boschstr. 12, D-69469 Weinheim, Germany

John Wiley & Sons Australia Ltd, 42 McDougall Street, Milton, Queensland 4064, Australia

John Wiley & Sons (Asia) Pte Ltd, 2 Clementi Loop #02-01, Jin Xing Distripark, Singapore 129809

John Wiley & Sons Canada Ltd, 6045 Freemont Blvd, Mississauga, Ontario, Canada L5R 4J3

Wiley also publishes its books in a variety of electronic formats. Some content that appears in print may not be available in electronic books.

Anniversary Logo Design: Richard J. Pacifico

British Library Cataloguing in Publication Data
A catalogue record for this book is available from the British Library

ISBN 978-0-470-98561-8 (HB)

Book design by Victoria Wong
Typeset by Random House, New York, USA.
Printed and bound in Great Britain by T.J. International Ltd, Padstow, Cornwall.
This book is printed on acid-free paper responsibly manufactured from sustainable forestry in which at least two trees are planted for each one used for paper production.

For my Chinese-speaking daughter,
Happy—my very best investment ever.

Do not wish for quick results, nor look for small advantages. If you seek quick results, you will not reach the ultimate goal. If you are led astray by small advantages, you will never accomplish great things.

—CONFUCIUS

A revolution is not a dinner party.

—MAO ZEDONG

CONTENTS

A BULL
IN CHINA

Introduction:
Catching the China Ride

Why invest in China?

After reading this book, I hope you'll agree that it still offers tremendous opportunities to the diligent investor in the century to come.

That's just what I said to myself way back in 1984, when I sought to become the first Westerner—maybe the first person ever—to ride a motorcycle across China. At the time, I'd earned enough as a cofounder of Quantum, a global investment fund, to sit in a Manhattan town house and count my dividends. But I've always been one of those adventuresome capitalists who would rather see, smell, and taste the real action than sit in a boardroom scanning graphs and charts.

Swapping my three-piece suit for a helmet and leathers, my ultimate aim was to make it around the world on my bike—while seeing as many changing societies and economies as I could put on my odometer. Getting to the Great Wall on my own set of wheels, and getting a read on one great big chunk of humanity, seemed the perfect escape from the pressures of Wall Street.

In the end, it took me more time and pit stops to get the many permits required by the Chinese than it took me to cross over three thousand miles from coastal Shanghai to the Karakoram Highway into bordering Pakistan. I suspect that I probably obtained all those official papers because nobody had ever dared ask to do something that weird.

My long ride was hardly a stroll through a teahouse. Roads turned to sand, or got washed out by floods. The detour signs weren't the sort I knew how to follow. Rocks bent my wheels, but spare parts were scarce and, at that time, so were decent Chinese restaurants—though the banquets were tasty when I found them. After too much riding gave me a stiff neck, a small-town doctor made me one of the first Western guinea pigs in China to get stuck with acupuncture needles. I was stopped by traffic cops more times than the Road Runner, had to weave safely past a nation of first-generation drivers, and once ran out of gas right in front of a top secret military base. Asking for a spare liter from the People's Liberation Army was tough, but they eventually did their bit to help me get down the road. However, I turned speechless at a fledgling disco in a small-town park when a polite young Chinese man asked me to be his partner for a fox-trot. Back then, few people were trotting out their business English, and the locals weren't sure what to make of a sandy-haired "foreign devil" from Alabama with no banjo on my knee but plenty of Gobi Desert dust on my face.

But I had such a blast that I crossed China again twice more, in 1990 by motorcycle, and nine years later in a customized Mercedes car as part of an epic three-year trip that covered 152,000 miles to celebrate the millennium. Each time I returned to Chinese soil, I felt like I was coming to an entirely new country. I eventually saw how all my assumptions about the fast-changing People's Republic had been plain wrong. I figured that the Chinese and I were complete opposites: the brash individualist tasting the freedom of the open road and championing unrestrained markets, versus group-minded, state-controlled, godless Communists.

That last one got put to rest on one of the very first nights of one journey. Checking into a hotel in the Muslim Far West, I saw a banner strung across the lobby that read, HOUSE OF GOD. Besides, I knew that if the people who ran China were giving an unrepentant Yankee trader like me the chance to run loose, something fundamental had to be changing.

I wish I could say that I was out there scouting for start-ups or great penny stocks. But I did tell anyone who would listen that these folks just might be presiding over one thriving economy within twenty years. In 1978, China's supreme leader, Deng Xiaoping, had restarted traditions of commerce suppressed for decades by wars, civil strife, and Communist dogma. So my cruises afforded me a terrific ground-level view of the "capitalist road" China was starting down. China's stock markets weren't open for business as yet, but real markets — the kinds where people buy a fish or a yard of silk — showed me how peasants were already tasting the fruits of deregulation and free enterprise. The way the price of watermelons kept fluctuating before reaching the proper level of supply and demand, and the way sellers haggled over them, made me wish I could have bought myself some melon futures.

Suddenly, the Chinese were forging their own careers and charting how to pursue a better life for their children. The amazing potential and entrepreneurial spirit of a billion people had been unleashed. I never got over the excitement of hearing a new restaurant owner speak proudly of meeting his payrolls, or returning to find a farmer's savings invested in his own carpet factory, watching kids who earned money from pool tables on the side of the open road moving on to bigger enterprises, or seeing one acquisitive peasant become "the orchard king" after buying up every plot of apples in his region. And making it all more exciting was the way people everywhere were reconnecting with traditions that for centuries had helped China lead the world's trade, science, and innovation.

I can't claim all my forays made me a true "China hand." Maybe just a China foot. Nor was I ever one of those goo-goo-eyed believers made giddy by the prospect of a billion-plus paying customers. As recently as 2004, when Chinese stock prices were still in the doldrums, weighed down by state-held shares and excess regulation, I spoke so pessimistically about investing that a national TV program out of Beijing censored my remarks.

Still, a conviction I acquired by the seat of my pants—and confirmed over time with hard, cold numbers—has led me to invite you to hop aboard an even more profitable journey. There will surely be rough patches on that journey, but I am convinced that those who ride them out will see real long-term gains. Actually, those rough patches will provide the most buying opportunities for investors—so the rougher, the better.

You could say that this book has been twenty-three years and over fifteen thousand miles in the making. So I hope you will use it as your road map to investment earnings in China. As one Chinese proverb says, "If you wish to know the way ahead, ask those who have traveled it."

When I first glimpsed the skylines of Chinese cities, they were drab and empty, dotted with a few Soviet-style spires. By 1990, they were clogged with construction cranes (Shanghai alone had a majority of those in use around the globe). These days, you don't see so many because the foundations of a modern powerhouse have already been laid. Now the world gets the fun of seeing what's going to rise upon them. And finally, after years of stutter steps, the same thing is happening with China's stock markets.

For nearly three decades, China has been the fastest-growing country in the world. With a rate of savings and investment exceeding 35 percent among its 1.3 billion people, and foreign reserves that already top the planet, it is set to become the most important country in mankind's future.

I'll go a step further: just as the nineteenth century belonged to England and the twentieth century to America, so the twenty-first century will be China's turn to set the agenda and rule the roost. Before I get into a single stock listing, the very best advice of any kind that I can give you is to teach your children or your grandchildren Chinese. It is going to be the most important language of their lifetimes.

Looking at China today, I see a whole lot of room for upward growth in Chinese industry, including power and energy, tourism and media, agriculture, infrastructure, high-tech—and I'll highlight those that could turn out to be the most "recession-proof." For those willing to put aside old prejudices and put in the time, the future AT&T's, Microsofts, and General Motors are waiting to be discovered. No wonder I'm a bull when it comes to this China shop.

In what follows, I'll explain in detail the mechanics of purchasing shares in China's ever-increasing legion of listed companies. I'll run through the handiest means to pick up the best bargains in Shanghai, Shenzhen, Hong Kong, or even New York, right from your corner broker. On the surface, China's numerous exchanges and multilayered regulations can appear daunting. So I'll try to make clear China's initially confusing A-shares and B-shares, and I'll recite the ABC's of secondary tools such as ADR's (American Depositary Receipts, a common way for foreign companies to access U.S. markets that makes it easier for Americans to invest in China). I'll dot the i's when assessing the country's quickening procession of seemingly irresistible IPO's (initial public offerings). Above all, I want to reduce the intimidation factor, and make sure that, when it comes to your money, nothing gets lost in translation.

Along the way, I'll offer my analysis of China's economy and outline the dynamics that drive earnings and innovation. I'm going to run down the significant government policies that affect domestic industries and global markets—as laid out in the latest Five-Year Plan, which is put out by China's rulers and is the basic blueprint for the country. And I intend to show both individual and institutional investors the way to benefit from emerging trends only China-watchers can glimpse. Where it matters, I'll analyze the World Trade Organization (WTO) framework that China entered into in 2001. In many cases, the changes in regulation, the reduction of tariffs, and the promises of greater market access for foreign firms are just beginning to shape competition in fields like banking, media, and telecommunications. In 2001, some hard-liners warned that lowering many trade barriers would harm the domestic economy—but it seems liberalized rules for imports and exports have only opened up more business for both sides and have spurred innovation within China's more stodgy industries.

In handy easy-to-clip "Sino Files," I'll introduce some of the exciting new enterprises that are rising along with the new China. I'll offer listing codes, basic reads on profit/revenue trends, and the relevant background for each enterprise. Some companies are already well-established industry leaders; others are just feeling their way into emerging markets. Many are showing dazzling fundamentals; most still have a long way to go. All are meant to be examples rather than specific picks or recommendations. Foreign companies that benefit significantly from China's expansion will be cited as well, but they won't be my main thrust. I'd rather familiarize you with the potential value of enterprises whose names you've never heard and may find hard to pronounce. Almost all show bottom lines that are easy to add up.

I'll likewise look at what the future may hold by scanning China's history, recent and ancient, for clues about China's goals and the country's methods for reaching them. But I will not shirk from taking a hard look at potential pitfalls, whether they involve geopolitical tensions or environmental threats.

This book isn't meant as some throwaway guide to yesterday's sure bets. I won't be revealing which stocks I hold personally, not just because I consider that a conflict of interest but because the world already has enough blind followers. Instead of offering you the whens and wheres that should be up to each individual investor, I'll give you the hows and whys that will help you share in China's amazing growth trajectory.

In my previous book, *Hot Commodities,* I showed how numbers that didn't reflect real supply-and-demand guaranteed a long-term two-decade bull market in a whole class of investments most people ignore. Commodities also happen to be a great way to profit from China's expansion, since the country's growing demand for everything from copper and nickel to soybeans and oil will be driving world prices for years to come. Owning a piece of the things that China's hot economy simply can't do without guarantees less need to worry about governments, management, or pension funds. And if you own commodities, the Chinese will always pay you on time.

But in this book, I want to outline a far broader range of choices for sharing in China's future. As I did for the commodities market, I want to point folks toward another market at the start of a very long upward ride—no matter the obstacles encountered along the way.

Just in case you are wondering, my confidence isn't based on nostalgia for my road trips. Unless you've taken monastic vows or spent the last decade under a rock, you are probably aware that China's opening to the world has led to the greatest economic boom since England's Industrial Revolution.

A Chinese friend who lived through all this commented, "The country has zoomed up from practically the financial bottom. In 1980, right before the dawn of the economic reform, China's GDP per capita weighted in purchasing power parity was a mere US$410, compared to US$12,230 at the time in the U.S. While the world economy enjoyed decades-long growth after World War II, we Chinese were in total isolation; doors closed while they attempted a socialist utopia. No private ownership, as everything belonged to the state. No free enterprise, as everything was centrally controlled. No competition, as food, clothes, even cooking oil, were allocated, usually barely enough for survival. No service industry, as you should always serve the people, not have yourself served. Changing jobs, professions, employers, or initiating anything new was impossible since your status was fixed from the moment you were born. No capital markets, as capital was branded a source of evil. That's why no other leap in our lifetimes can be as astounding as this one."

With a growth rate averaging 9 percent since the start of the 1980s, the value of the Chinese economy has pretty much doubled each decade, and shows few signs of stopping.

If projections hold, China will surpass the United States as the world's largest economy within twenty to thirty years. On top of that, China attracted nearly US$70 billion in direct foreign investment during 2006, which, combined with its trade surplus, has brought Beijing's foreign-currency reserves above US$1.3 trillion (now the largest in the world). In one astounding decade, China's manufacturing base for durable goods increased one hundredfold.

But all those heavy numbers are just a starting point. Sleek office towers and assembly lines rising from rice paddies don't mean as much as China's immeasurable advances in civil conduct, internationalized awareness, and opportunities for achievement. In urban areas, the traditional greeting "Have you eaten today?" has been replaced by "Have you surfed the Net today?" Chinese executives, engineers, artists, athletes, and designers are already leading the world into "the Chinese century."

Right now, the place reminds me a whole lot of America in the late 1800s, when the United States emerged onto the world stage after civil war and political turmoil. That was the era of the so-called robber barons, with booming new cities like Chicago, and the invention of defining technologies like the telephone and the lightbulb along with major international companies like Standard Oil. It was a time of unbridled expansion and enterprise and the formation of key industries. Then, too, there were plenty of concerns to scare off investors: assassinations of presidents, race riots, labor unrest and civil strife, few human rights, several economic depressions, corrupt government and business practices. That is right where China is today: a Wild East comparable to that Wild West. Imagine how uncertain America's future appeared to the world in 1908; China seems just as chaotic and fraught with challenges today. But looking at the direction in American investments from 1908 to 2007 gives me a lot of confidence in the China of 2008. In 1907, in fact, the U.S. economy collapsed and the naysayers were jubilant. But even those who bought at the top back then came out way, way ahead.

Jumping on the bandwagon—especially one this big—has never been my style. It's when I've moved away from the crowd that I've usually made my best investments. At the time of this writing, Chinese stocks are up since the bear-market bottom in 2005. While a bubble may loom in certain sectors and we may even see a dramatic correction, we need to prepare ourselves for long-term opportunities, of which there will be many.

Do you want to share in the growth of burgeoning Beijing-based corporations? Profit from the increased purchasing power of the biggest middle class the world has ever seen? Participate in China's enormous potential for consumer goods, or maybe solid industrial exports? Or would you like to have a stake in Chinese efforts to develop cities and real estate? Or lend a hand in the creation of the first great Chinese wine? Do you want to trade in currency when that's an option? Maybe you want to invest in a Chinese commodities company to benefit from both demand and supply, or an agricultural company that's being boosted by new government supports. The possibilities are as limitless as the country itself.

Now is the time to engage China and all things Chinese. Go there if you can, or if you've already climbed the Great Wall, go back again to see the great changes. Even at home, you could take a class in tai chi and then learn about Chinese medicine. Read some of the many good books about life in contemporary China. See their movies. The point is to develop a clear sense of how Chinese people view the world and lead their lives. Try to figure out how China's consumers will spend *their* hard-earned cash and where they might put it to make it grow.

I'm such a believer in China's long-term prospects that I brought in a Chinese nanny to rear my daughter, Happy, born in 2003 and already a happy Mandarin speaker. As I've counseled before and will counsel again: get out of the dollar, teach your children Chinese, and buy commodities.

Then call on your homegrown experience and discerning eye to find emerging Chinese brands with competitive advantage. Suppose you are an auto mechanic. You probably know an enormous amount about cars and engines, and the relative value of certain models or design breakthroughs. So I would suggest examining China's auto industry to find something you believe in. If you're a hairdresser, you might have a feel for fashion brands or cosmetics. Just remember: you know a whole lot more about these things than any Wall Street brokers.

To guide your own route to riches in China, you've got to use your own passion and initiative. Maybe you'll spot the next Chinese "red chip" with decades of upside to come. Do the math and don't treat China any differently from anyplace else. Be skeptical and stay with what you know. The success stories in life are people who figure out what they know, stay with it, and watch it very carefully. Only you can know the way to become your own bull in China.

Let me emphasize: this is not a catalog of hot tips or even of recommendations. Rather, it is my survey of business happenings in China. The companies discussed may or may not be successful. They are just some of the most intriguing starting points I know to get you going on your own homework. By following your instincts and knowing the numbers, you will probably discover Chinese enterprises and industries not even hinted at here.

When my generation was growing up, our parents warned us that China was the place where you would end up if you kept digging a hole in the sand. It was the opposite end of the earth. There are a lot of "experts" out there who still make a living frightening people about a country that was, in recent memory, our ideological enemy. Investors should be cautious, but fear of the unknown and the foreign should not hold people back. Now is not the time to stick our heads in the sand.

Since I began planning my first China cruise, the world has moved quicker than any Harley-Davidson. Communist slogans are as old hat as Mao caps. Even in Vietnam, booms have replaced battles. India, too, has emerged from Indira Gandhi's "emergency" to cast off its isolation. In less than half my lifetime, three billion Asians have become part of the world economy. In terms of finance, the center has moved even more dramatically. In 2002, twenty-three of the world's twenty-five largest IPO's were on Wall Street. In 2006, it was down to just one.

Sometimes embracing the obvious requires the most difficult change in mind-set. People have been staring at China's indicators for years. But few outside the country have really been willing to accept an objective, long-term view—or been able to shed the comfort they get from looking at world geography in a fixed way (with the United States at the center). At the very least, investors can achieve diversification and much-needed protection from future U.S. weakness, just as I have done by putting my own funds in twenty-eight foreign markets. Maybe it's all about heeding the wisdom of Confucius, who warned twenty-five hundred years ago, "If a man takes no thought about what is distant, he will find sorrow near at hand."

Just as I did with the commodities market, I'm challenging all of us to take a hard look and see what's in front of our noses. And China couldn't be any closer than the nearest beach ball or blanket. If you still need convincing, take a survey of the items in your house right now, from electronics to clothes, printed books to toys, and see how many read MADE IN CHINA.

Why shouldn't you make something from that? To cite another ancient Chinese saying, "There's a day to dry your nets and a day to cast your nets."

Now is the time for preparing your nets.

I'd like to end this Introduction with a note of caution. The Chinese government is, as I write this, continuing to confront concerns over a bubble, and it's uncertain what the immediate future will bring. Perhaps stocks will decline and produce a soft landing, giving us all immediate opportunities. However, *if* a full bubble develops, I recommend a period of caution. Read this book, learn as much as you can about the Chinese market, and be ready to move when things bottom out. Luck goes to the prepared mind!

1

Investing: From Mao Caps
to Small-Market Caps

Two stock markets, three if you count Hong Kong's. At least five types of shares, not to mention ADR's and various funds. Shares you can purchase outside China that you can't if you are there, and shares with differing values on different exchanges. Like most everything else about China, buying into China's prosperity is loads more complicated than it needs to be but a whole lot simpler than it looks from a distance. And the process is getting ever more accessible to foreign investors through U.S. brokers, international banks, and the Internet. So do not let the details deter you: a stock is a stock, a solid company worth investing in, no matter where it is listed. But before you decide how to invest, let's review the way China's exchanges have been forged—and just where they may be headed in future.

How China Took Stock

Forget pandas or golden pagodas. On my third journey to China in 1988, the first Chinese attraction I wanted to see for myself was a small trading counter that had recently been set up by the Industrial and Commercial Bank of China. This wasn't quite a real stock market yet. Without tickers or brokers, the few shares traded there—at the start in late 1986, just thirty a day, representing two companies, not exactly major volume—were practically done by appointment. Though Shanghai had once hosted the richest exchange in Asia, it would still take two more years to launch properly once more. Yet this nondescript office, in a small building off an unpaved side street strewn with piles of water pipes, made the workings of capitalism more vividly real to me than all the world's speeding electronic tickers. Here was honest-to-goodness "over the counter" buying and selling— across one single cluttered counter, in fact.

Having found the place, which a government official had mentioned to me in passing, I couldn't resist joining a few brave souls in purchasing stock certificates, printed on real paper as oversize as my high school diploma. Nothing "virtual" here. With the help of my translator, and the few stray old gentlemen in line who remembered the old exchanges from before 1949 and were adding some excitement to their old age, I attempted to place my own order across an open ledge to a poor lady clerk who nearly went into shock. She seemed afraid to take my money—Chinese bills, as good as anyone else's—and had to confer with superiors since I was the first "foreign ghost" to turn up before her. Even after she agreed with a grin to finalize the trade, the stock itself, and numerous torn receipts flimsy as flypaper, had to be passed around for numerous "chops"—official carved seals wielded by bureaucrats. This was followed by so much clicking and reclicking of beads on a desktop abacus that I had to tell them to move it and complete the transaction before my stock price moved up.

But I was proud when it all got done. For an inveterate investor, holding a piece of China's burgeoning experiment in free markets was a lot more exciting than grasping chopsticks. "May we all get rich together!" I told the clerk, two years ahead of the real Shanghai exchange's opening. The twinkle in her eye indicated she just might have understood.

I wish I could claim that single share of an obscure bank is now worth all the tea in Shanghai. I have no idea. Nor do I want to know.

It is framed and hanging on my wall. It will probably be more valuable as an antique someday than as a stock. In any case, I'll never sell it, as they told me I was the first foreigner ever to buy there. But I can assure you that China's "experiment" in stock exchanges has more than panned out. In the first twelve years, listed companies rose from twelve to nearly fourteen hundred, investors in Chinese exchanges rose from four hundred thousand to just under sixty-seven million—and that was before things really took off at the end of 2005! From 1991 to 2005, companies raised over US$150 billion on the two exchanges. By September 2006, the two exchanges listed 1,377 companies, with total market capitalization of US$400 billion.

Despite wasted years of inconsistent policies, reflecting a lack of experience and a lack of faith in market mechanisms, the Shanghai Stock Exchange (established along with one in the booming southern border town of Shenzhen) has already become the second-highest in capitalization for Asia, at *over* US$500 billion, on its way to returning to the place of preeminence it held before the Second World War.

Actually, the Chinese have been capitalists since way back. If the capitalist system itself is one of the few inventions that the Chinese can't claim, they certainly have plenty of practice at private entrepreneurship—and, given time, may yet perfect it. Even during the last decadent days of the Qing Dynasty (1644–1911), when antiquated feudal rule under the aging empress dowager left China open for plunder by Western armies, some Chinese companies began issuing public shares as a means to raise money for expansion. In the late 1860s, a securities trading market started up in Shanghai. A list of thirteen companies, including the Hongkong and Shanghai Banking Corporation (global HSBC as we know it today), appeared in a June 1866 newspaper under the "Shares and Stocks" section. (The New York Stock Exchange had started small, too, in 1792.)

The first share trading firm was established in Shanghai as early as 1882. In 1891, during a boom in mining shares, European and American businessmen founded the Shanghai Share Broker's Association, China's first stock exchange, to help make stocks available to foreigners in that thriving international settlement. By 1914, China's government had passed the first regulatory law concerning securities. Small trading counters were established in the northern cities of Tianjin and Beijing. But Shanghai's main exchange dominated from 1920 and thrived through the thirties, when Shanghai, divided into British, French, and American zones, reached its wild apex as the "Paris of the East." In 1937, Japanese bombardment and occupation put a definite end to all investment and speculation frenzies. While small exchanges were attempted in the chaotic days before and after the Communist Party's takeover in 1949, anything resembling shareholding or trading vanished for three decades of collectivization and economic control and ownership by Mao Zedong's omnipresent state.

During the fanatical period of the Cultural Revolution, Chinese people were persecuted for reading Western novels or knowing how to play the piano. Can you imagine how much sludge someone would have had to shovel to do penance for holding a share of IBM? Years of forced labor would have awaited anyone even caught mumbling about such horrid things as brokerage firms or initial public offerings (if anyone in China had even heard of them). But in July 1977, just one year after the end of a decade of tumult that left China poorer and more isolated than ever, Deng Xiaoping, a former vice president and general of the Red Army who had been living under house arrest, was restored to his party posts and would soon start the country on a path of pragmatism and reform.

The Communist system, Deng could clearly see, was failing worldwide. A quick look at the world in the 1980s confirmed that countries permitting competition, allowing low-tariff imports of raw materials and intermediate goods, and encouraging exports through realistic currency values were doing well. The "Asian Tigers" of South Korea, Taiwan, Hong Kong, and Singapore inspired Deng to offer his famed dictum: "It doesn't matter if a cat is black or white so long as it catches mice." The cat turned out to be capitalism, prosperity its prey. In the meantime, the country was going to need a lot more than government alone could provide to rebuild and expand its base. As Deng would later muse publicly, "Are such things as securities and stock markets good or not? Are they dangerous? It is permitted to try them out, but it must be done with determination."

Some people were determined to get going right away, especially after Deng permitted farmers freed from their communal duties to sell small crops in order to improve equipment. That was in 1984, the year of my first meanderings, and I can't say that I saw too much trading in anything but old Mao caps. Several years earlier, some factories and department stores had begun raising capital the old-fashioned way, testing the limits of what was permissible. By 1986, Deng Xiaoping actually welcomed the head of the New York Stock Exchange to the Great Hall of the People! His original plan was to experiment with stock issuance in Shenzhen, since he'd tried out almost every other facet of the new system. This farming village on China's southern border with Hong Kong boomed into a prosperous city of six million after it was designated the first "Special Economic Zone." In 1988, the Shenzhen Development Bank, born of numerous credit unions, was allowed to sell five hundred thousand shares of common stock—that quickly and successfully raised several million in both U.S. and Hong Kong dollars.

But Shanghai, China's savvy window to the West since the mid-nineteenth century, was not to be denied its role. Rushed into existence by the need to find ways to raise funds at a time when money supplies had tightened to curb inflation, Shanghai's exchange opened in December 1990. Thousands waited in line for days to buy shares, though only eight companies were represented. Shenzhen, already operating, had its official launch six months later. To this day, the two exchanges both claim the distinction of having started first. Some temporary rules on stock issue and trading, cobbled together in 1989 from whatever overseas exchange rules the Chinese could translate, governed both.

Having seen its modest original site scant years before, I was stunned by my first peek at the current Shanghai exchange—now in Pudong, a futuristic city of skyscrapers set across the Huangpu River from the historic part of town. Here I saw at once how China's markets could take advantage of having studied existing markets and could leapfrog over all of them in the future. The setting was luxurious, the trading high-tech. There was none of the clutter and bother of live traders racing around like they still do in "backward" burgs like New York. No hand signals or confetti, just pure electronic trading—which is far speedier and more efficient. The building that houses the New York Stock Exchange, remember, was built in 1903, China's exchanges in 1990. One of those credited with an influential report that helped push China's leaders into taking that big step toward capitalism was a Chinese student named Wang Boming, who had returned from working five years at the Wall Street exchange.

In the beginning, regulators who held tight controls on which companies could list were concentrating mainly on aiding prestigious Hong Kong and New York IPO's for big state firms, and these regulators had little appreciation for the accountability that a free market demands. Amazingly, China had no laws to govern corporations until 1994 and no laws to regulate securities until 1999—nine years after the stock markets opened their doors. In spite of this lack of oversight, the number of individual stock investors exceeded ten million by the end of 1994.

The ride to prosperity has not been without its bumps and setbacks. At first, it seemed the market couldn't fail. Beginning in 1991, the Shanghai index went from 100 to 250 points in less than a year, and then reached 1,200 by the first quarter of 1992. By mid-1992, multiples of 50 to 100 times actual earnings became the norm on the Shanghai Stock Exchange and some "hot" issues fetched even higher multiples.

But by June 1992, the Shanghai stock market had dropped by more than 60 percent in a period of five months. Within a few days of hitting bottom, the bull market returned, and in just three months, the overall market index rose from 400 to a new height of 1,600. However, by the middle of 1994, the index was back to 400. From 1993 to 2001, the Shanghai market suffered twenty mini-crashes of more than 10 percent within a month.

During the first decade of operation, overall market growth seemed spectacular—but it was an illusion. Companies burned through the cash generated from splashy IPO's. Investment banks like Merrill Lynch were coming in and handing millions of dollars to companies on silver platters, shouting, "We want to invest!" Far from idiots, the Chinese thought it was great, and took the money to buy Rolexes and Ferraris. International Trust and Investment Corporations (ITIC's),

Chinese government-backed investment companies, had raised billions of dollars to develop much-needed Chinese infrastructure: airports, toll roads, seaports, and especially power plants. But these trusts made the age-old banker's mistake of lending long and borrowing short—and in 1999, some went bankrupt or had to be bailed out by the Chinese government, further damaging the credibility of China's business community. By 2001–2002, the fledgling securities industry also fell apart in scandal. Inevitably, as has been the case in every investment market throughout history, some people took advantage, getting the jump on those not in the know. This kind of behavior is as old as time and not just China's problem.

In this period, I had already started picking up bargains in China. In May 1999, for instance, B-shares available to foreigners were in such disrepute that they had fallen 85 percent from their highs. Such a discrepancy really whet my appetite—and I bought quite a few. But I stayed away after that until late 2005.

I knew China's investment mechanisms lagged behind the country's breakneck development largely because the mechanisms were dominated by creaky state-run enterprises that didn't have clear values, shareholder rights, or transparent accounting. Of course, every stock market in the world has nontradable shares such as company cross-holdings, government-owned shares, and private holdings. But while about 14 percent of shares worldwide are nontradable, 70 percent of the value of China's listed companies were in that category in 2002. Only 11 percent of listed companies were entirely outside government hands.

Figuring out how to reduce this overhang, and how to do so in a fair manner for other stockholders, has been a major hurdle. Faced with an explosion of available shares, any market is at risk of a collapse. The Tracker Fund of Hong Kong, the first exchange-traded fund (ETF) in the Asia Pacific, was originally created as a vehicle for the Hong Kong government to unload the shares it bought to maintain market stability during the financial turmoil in 1998. Each quarter since its launch in November 1999, the Hong Kong market has seen a drop when the government has put those shares on the market.

In 2001, one flawed plan to deal with China's state-held shares caused an immediate 45 percent crash. Doubt and anxiety increased when each new plan was floated—then dashed—regarding how to re-calculate value once this flood of new shares was released. So tradable volume listed on China's two exchanges declined by nearly 30 percent between 2001 and 2004. No wonder, then, that even as China's economy went ballistic, stocks stayed in the doldrums. A lot of value was represented but too many stocks with uncertain disposal plans were hanging over the market.

On a trip to China in 2004, I was a featured guest on *Dialogue,* one of China Central Television's flagship programs. Instead of presenting the rosy perspective interviewers expected, I predicted that China's exchanges—already in the doldrums of a very bearish mood since 2001—would decline even further for another year or so. As I already mentioned, a lot of my fellow guests got indignant. I heard later that the producers delayed airing the segment. Eventually though, they did broadcast my comments, after the market tanked as I'd predicted and was headed for the recovery I'd predicted as well.

During that same trip, I gave a talk to Shanghai business school students on closed-circuit TV. After I made similarly discouraging re-marks, I got into a debate with a professor who accused me of single-handedly trying to manipulate Chinese markets. This showed he was pretty naïve about investing, in general, and about just how much power one investor can have, in specific. But this sort of reaction wasn't particularly Chinese, a special by-product of some sinister pro-paganda machine. I'm used to taking unpopular stands regarding the market, and used to the disbelief and outrage that comes from bro-kers and analysts and market officials who, after all, have a vested in-terest in being optimistic and selling that optimism like soap to their clients. There's another Chinese proverb that goes, "A melon-seller never cries 'bitter melons,' nor a wine-seller 'thin wine.' " Markets, in their book, are always meant to head upward.

When even market managers and government officials made de-spairing remarks, I had a feeling things couldn't get much worse. I be-came bullish in the fall of 2005 after the Chinese government had finally stepped in with decisive reforms. Most important of these was a new requirement that companies with large stakes held by the state had to compensate public shareholders by issuing them additional shares in the companies. Then I began buying again.

As of mid-2006, less than 50 percent of shares were state-owned, a dramatic improvement considering that in January 2002, the state owned 78 percent of equity shares. Through measured negotiations and provisions, significant progress has been made, and the government is clearly on track to meet its stated goal of floating all nontradable shares.

After stocks started climbing in the summer of 2005, the Shanghai exchange went from around 1,000 index points to 4,000 by July 2007. But that hardly means that the stock market reflects the full value of the private sector in China. Even after a period of market fever, and millions of new investors in 2007—a sign of confidence more than worry—the market remains relatively small in terms of its role in the greater economy (raising about 10 percent of the capital needed for China's growth).

Finally, China's markets may be in the hands of professionals. China's equivalent of the Securities and Exchange Commission, the China Securities Regulatory Commission (CSRC), is now full of smart managers with exceptional knowledge of markets and laws in Western countries. Of course, every stock exchange has its problems. There will be slips and stumbles ahead, as there are in any markets. With huge amounts of money involved, there will be backdoor temptations and maneuvering. This isn't the volunteer fire department we're talking about.

"Crossing the river by feeling the stones in front of you," was how Deng Xiaoping, China's prophet of profit making, described the country's process of reform. Today, the river of doubt has nearly been crossed.

When I first went to China, it would have been unimaginable to think electronic exchanges would even be established, or that the aforementioned "foreign devils" would be allowed a significant stake in their progress. Now, after decades of trial and error, the very symbol of a free market economy—the stock exchange—has proven its worth as an engine for driving the necessary formation of capital and the public participation of "the masses" in the creation of new wealth. Karl Marx couldn't have drawn it up better.

Chinese Alphabet Soup

If you think buying Chinese stocks is confusing, you should have tried mailing a postcard in China back in the 1980s. Traditionally, China has required a lot of paperwork to do most anything. The aim is control—never let anything get out of hand on your watch. The Communist Party's ongoing legitimacy rests on holding together the disparate interests and regions of the country, maintaining the stability that has allowed amazing growth.

But how do you control free markets that, after all, have to get a little out of control in order to do their job? And how do you raise funds for your companies without letting some of the wrong interests, even foreign interests, buy their way into your economy?

The answer, for the Chinese, is a "split-share" system that allows Chinese companies to issue different classes of shares to domestic and foreign investors. It's an unwieldy, yet workable, compromise that keeps investors coming while making the government's economic watchdogs feel relatively secure. Even as these watchdogs still give lip service to building "socialism with Chinese characteristics," so they have created a capitalist stock market in a decidedly Chinese manner that tries, through trying layers of complexity, to ensure that the common people of the People's Republic get first crack at the country's corporate future.

So here's how to read China's current version of alphabet soup:

A-Shares

Listed on Shanghai and Shenzhen exchanges. On an individual basis, these are available to domestic Chinese investors only. They are denominated in renminbi, not freely convertible to international currencies. Since November 2002, QFII's (Qualified Foreign Institutional

Investors), such as large banks, funds, and securities companies with at least US$10 billion in management, have been allowed to buy up to 10 percent of a company's shares (still held in Chinese currency). While such investors have an impact on the overall market, this belated invitation to join the party, approved after a long downward trend in China's stock prices, doesn't give the average investor access to these stocks. Mainly large institutions buy these shares. However, regulations change fast, and holders of B-shares could find them swapped for A-shares at some point, so all these listings are important to watch and consider. Sooner or later, Chinese markets will be open to all, just as they are in the United States and other developed nations.

B-Shares

This class of shares was first created in the mid-1990s to be sold solely to foreigners using foreign currency. At that time, Chinese companies were attracted to the idea because foreigners eager to invest in China were at first willing to pay more per share than their domestic counterparts. So a bubble developed—but eventually popped, until people were practically giving away B-shares—which is why I started buying them in May 1999.

In 2001, the Chinese government gave their citizens access to B-shares if they could show that they were starting accounts for foreigners. So money flooded in from overseas Chinese—and more than three quarters of the stocks jumped the daily limit of a 10 percent rise in price that had been set to establish "orderly markets." That was before regulators started worrying more about how to slow overheated exchanges.

B-shares are denominated in Hong Kong dollars on the Shenzhen exchange and in U.S. dollars on the Shanghai exchange. Generally speaking, due to lower demand, the long-term performance of the B-share market has lagged far behind the A-share market—even when the same company issues A-shares and B-shares with identical voting and dividend rights. From 1993 to 2000, A-share prices averaged 420 percent higher than their B-share counterparts.

And B-shares remain primarily for individual foreign investors. Many companies don't bother to issue them, just as many Chinese won't touch them because they continue to have the stigma of somehow being "foreign." This could perhaps lead to opportunities since many B-shares may eventually be merged with the A-share market.

H-Shares

If most A-shares are available only to Chinese investors and qualified foreign institutional investors, there's a handy alternative. Many of China's best A-list companies have previously preferred the prestige and fund-raising potential of listing abroad — and that usually means listing in familiar Hong Kong. Sometimes companies can sell at better prices on foreign exchanges than at home; at other times, companies simply benefit from the exposure. Although foreign listing is a common practice for companies in countries such as South Africa and Israel, Chinese companies have by far the most listings overseas — beginning in Hong Kong. Shares listed outside China are freely open to all foreigners. The largest block of these are H-shares listed on the Stock Exchange of Hong Kong, in Hong Kong dollars (fully convertible). China Mobile, China Unicom, CNOOC (China National Offshore Oil Corporation), and Legend are all leading Chinese components of Hong Kong stock exchange's Hang Seng Index.

Before 1997, when Hong Kong was reabsorbed into China as a special administrative region, the main goal of top-status Chinese firms, especially state-owned enterprises, was to get approval for an IPO in Hong Kong. After negotiations between the Hong Kong exchange head and then Chinese vice premier Zhu Rongji, Tsingtao Beer became the first Chinese company listed in Hong Kong in 1993. And many of China's biggest companies, the so-called red chips, with at least 30 percent mainland ownership, soon followed. A recent change in China's Qualified Domestic Institutional Investor scheme (not to be confused with the structure for foreign investors, mentioned above) will allow large Chinese banks and institutions to invest up to 50 percent overseas — so that should bring more big buyers into Hong Kong's market as well. Now China's State Administration of Foreign Exchange (SAFE) has announced a pilot scheme to allow mainland residents to invest directly in Hong Kong, which should eventually bring a flood of mainland capital into Hong Kong–listed stocks.

Foreign listings also give Chinese companies more freely available equity to use for future acquisitions. In October 2006, China Construction Bank Corporation became the first of the big four state-owned banks to list offshore in this manner, with a US$9.2 billion Hong Kong initial public offering. The largest of the big four, the Industrial and Commercial Bank of China, executed a US$21.9 billion deal listing on both the Hong Kong stock exchange and the Shanghai exchange in October 2006. At the time, that was the largest IPO ever.

S-Shares

This refers to shares sold on the Singapore exchange. While far-off in Southeast Asia, hyperprosperous and defiantly capitalist Singapore has a majority Chinese population and has always maintained close links with China. As of 2006, over 14 percent of the listings on the Singapore exchange were Chinese companies — as Singapore has been aggressive in trying to lure mainland brethren. Besides, prosperous Singaporeans have more money to spend on stocks than investors in many other countries. A number of Singapore-based venture capital firms with big holdings in China are also listed here. All S-shares are freely tradable and convertible, as is the Singapore dollar.

N-Shares and ADR's

This refers to Chinese companies listed directly on the New York Stock Exchange or the NASDAQ. In 1999, China.com listed on the NASDAQ, as did Sina.com. A U.S. listing has traditionally been considered prestigious and once brought higher prices. But now Asians tend to drive their own prices high enough and IPO's are a lot more expensive to mount in the United States, so U.S. listings suffered for a while — and may slow due to newly enacted Chinese regulations aimed at encouraging companies to list at home. However, at last count, there were forty-three Chinese companies on the NASDAQ and twenty-two on the NYSE, but projected to soon hit thirty-five.

Another way that a Chinese company can list abroad is to sell shares from an initial issue on a mainland or Hong Kong exchange to an investment bank, which then will act as the intermediary and underwrite American Depositary Receipts (ADR) on a foreign exchange against their holdings of the original listing. It is easy to find the Chinese companies available through ADR's. As of 2006, there were thirty-three Chinese ADR's trading on the NASDAQ—the main over-the-counter system in America—and sixteen Chinese ADR's trading on the New York Stock Exchange.

L-Shares

Many international exchanges are eager to attract business and publicity through Chinese company listings, and the London Stock Exchange announced in late 2006 that it would step up its efforts to attract listings from Chinese companies—though they, too, may be affected by the new regulations in China. They have six Chinese companies so far, but the smaller Alternative Investment Market (AIM) board in London has long been a destination for Chinese companies, with forty-six current listings.

J-Shares

In April 2007, Asia Media Co., a Beijing-based provider of TV program guides, became the first Chinese company to get listed on the Tokyo Stock Exchange's market for emerging companies. Nineyou International, an online game software developer, then listed on the Osaka exchange. So Japan may become another place to look.

OTCBB

There are thousands of more obscure companies, frequently penny stocks, that don't meet NASDAQ's listing requirements. These companies trade separately, often with their prices listed only once daily, on the Over-the-Counter Bulletin Board, sometimes referred to as Pink Sheets. This is a daily publication compiled by the National Quotation Bureau and contains price quotations for Over-the-Counter stocks in the United States. Many Chinese stocks can be traded there.

STAQ and NET

In addition to the Shanghai and Shenzhen exchanges, China has nationwide over-the-counter systems. The first is a computerized trading structure called the Securities Trading Automated Quotations system, modeled on NASDAQ in the United States. The STAQ system is the world's largest computerized trading method, as ranked by number of computer outlets. The second, the National Electronic Trading System, trades Chinese treasury bonds and shares owned by state-owned enterprises. These will eventually be open to all investors.

You could look at all this as an impossible playing field, or as a glut of means to the same end. There are some strange wrinkles in such a system: an individual foreigner would be prohibited from buying A-shares in a company listed in China, but could buy B-, H-, L-, N-, J-, or S-shares in the same company. Interestingly enough, Chinese domestic investors bear the brunt of the risk in China's developing market since they can invest only at home while most foreigners have more choices. That's why, when manias develop on the mainland, prices there will go to big premiums for the same shares abroad.

Until a few years ago, China would not allow its citizens to exchange renminbi for foreign currencies. The only foreign currency that domestic investors could legally obtain was money sent back from overseas relatives or friends. Furthermore, many of China's more mature and profitable companies are not available to domestic investors because the companies are listed on overseas exchanges. While mainland Chinese are the customers, suppliers, producers, and even employees of these companies, they are barred from investing in them.

Over the past decade and a half, the Shanghai and Shenzhen exchanges have developed distinct identities. Many of the large, state-owned companies are now listed on the Shanghai Stock Exchange. This is where you want to be to raise big bucks or gain prestige. Shenzhen lists more export-oriented companies, joint ventures, and newer start-ups, making it more of a place to gamble on the unusual. Initially, the government intended Shenzhen to be the primary board competing against and maintaining close links with the more established Hong Kong exchange just a half-hour subway ride across the border. But since 1992, the Shanghai Stock Exchange has become many times more active.

Like Japan, China's stock market has leaned heavily toward the industrial sector, with many manufacturing-oriented companies. Based on the Dow Jones Global Classification Standard, as of June 2005, the industrial sector represented about 20 percent of the Dow Jones China index, much more than the Dow Jones world index's allocation of 11 percent. Other sectors allied to manufacturing have significant representation in China's stock market—combining to cover more than 70 percent of market capitalization. At the global level, those same sectors account for only about 36 percent.

China Mobile and China Unicom are both listed and traded in Hong Kong only. As a result, Hong Kong has been overly represented in telecommunication stocks (22.6 percent in 2006), when mainland China's telecommunications sector represents only 0.2 percent of its market. Likewise, CNOOC and Lenovo Holdings, leading companies in the energy and technology sectors, are listed only in Hong Kong, skewing the representation of those areas. However, with new regulations and increasing market balance, the impact of China Mobile has been decreasing. At last count, the thirty-eight Chinese companies issuing H-shares accounted for just over 13 percent of the value of the Hang Seng Index.

At the same time, the government sets the quota for new IPO's each year, selects the qualified companies based on provincial and sector allocation, and, until 2001, even determined where the new stocks would list. (No wonder there has been so much frenzy associated with these new listings, often purposely undervalued, with some rising seventeen times in a day!) China hasn't given up state control entirely: it's still the only country where the government limits the size of the stock market and the pace of new issues. That's one reason why investors grab up stocks for important new offerings. Also, under China's current laws, no company is allowed to list without three years of continuous profitability—a much more conservative policy than in the United States.

In 2005, Chinese state regulators actually stopped new IPO's altogether, in hopes that a decrease in stocks would drive up demand in what was then a weak market. When the CSRC started approving IPO's again in June 2006, sixty-five companies filed for IPO's in Shanghai and Shenzhen. In 2006, counting all overseas markets where Chinese companies file, eighty-six companies staged IPO's, raising over US$43 billion. Astonishingly, the average first-day jump for a Chinese A-share IPO was 78.27 percent in 2006; for the first four months of 2007, it was 106.90 percent. That can sound very tempting, but, of course, many shares are available only on secondary markets. My view, in general, is to stay away from frenzies and to look at IPO's if and when the boom declines. I never was one for flipping stocks immediately; my timing isn't that deft. I prefer to wait for a time when IPO's are more humdrum or even downright disregarded.

There is no special advantage or disadvantage to what letter of share one holds—except, of course, if you can find the same share at a lower price. Prices can and will fluctuate: for example, in early 2007, A-shares were just about double the price of B-shares and a third higher than H-shares—so it's definitely worth it to keep tabs on this. The bubble was even bigger on the mainland since Chinese could invest only at home. The more seasoned Hong Kongers had more choices about where to put their money and, unlike their mainland cousins, had seen a few more bubbles in their time. As I've said, many shares listed in both Hong Kong and the mainland are exactly the same except for where they are listed. The huge discounts in prices in Hong Kong may well disappear soon. Likewise, we should see the previous, comparatively lower prices for Chinese shares in Hong Kong rise as the mainland money seeks out cheaper Chinese stocks in Hong Kong and eventually everywhere they can be found.

And remember: due to such a divided system, company values are not as clearly correlated with earnings or even earnings potential in

China. Values can be driven down or up by different sets of investors and different rules and conditions. But don't be daunted. There are still plenty of outstanding stock choices available for any type of investor among Chinese B-shares, the Hong Kong, New York, Singapore, London, and Japanese exchanges.

Exchanging Old Ways for New

China's stock regulations are the result of many years' trial and error by bureaucrats who may or may not have known what was really best for free markets. Nobody would purposely run an exchange with a hodgepodge, and soon enough, rules and shares are bound to be standardized.

As China hurtles forward, predictions can seem outdated by the next morning. But the floating of state-owned shares, the first major hurdle in reforming the stock markets, has almost been cleared. Eliminating state ownership will turn the Chinese exchanges into truly free markets. Not only will this impact market liquidity, but it also decreases chances for corporate mismanagement and corruption. Individual shareholders hold companies accountable, allowing for a more accurate assessment of what company shares are worth.

The second great hurdle will be to restructure the split-share system in such a way as to encourage equal treatment of foreign capital—or to eliminate the system altogether. Initially constructed to prevent experienced foreigners from taking advantage of a nascent capitalist economy, it really serves little purpose now—especially as the Chinese themselves are the biggest speculators. All the hurdles to foreign share purchases ought to be eliminated so that there's a level playing field for all. China has no reason to fear open markets any longer.

In a turnaround, some Chinese firms are moving out to buy up shares and make takeover bids on American and European companies. Ultimately, if the Chinese want the right to move their capital freely abroad, they will have to grant such freedom to foreigners in return. And regulators on the mainland are already beginning to take this new reality into account. Already, the Qualified Foreign Institutional Investor scheme, allowing institutional foreign investors to become the second most influential block on the exchange, after mutual funds, is set to be further expanded (possibly increasing from an entrance quota of US$10 billion to US$40 billion at the end of 2007).

Next, a solution to the problem of "second-class" B-shares will have to follow. How to do this with minimal disruption remains at the top of the CSRC's agenda. One approach will be to set formulas for state-held companies to compensate minority shareholders, as has been done with A-shares. The second approach, and the simpler, would be to abolish the B-share market altogether by converting B-shares to A-shares. This would mean all shares would be open to all types of investors, as on all other major markets. Already, it's been announced that the barriers for institutional investors buying A-shares are going to be liberalized, allowing more foreign influence. So that's a good sign.

In March 2007, Hu Xiaolian, administrator of the State Administration of Foreign Exchange (SAFE), announced that her board is contemplating an arbitrage scheme between A-shares and Hong Kong's H-share market, due to the growing discrepancy between the two. If initiated, this would link markets in Hong Kong and the mainland much more closely in terms of prices and general coordination. Arbitraging means buying and selling in different places, playing one value against another, until adjusted demand brings them in line.

Looking ahead, it also seems highly probable that someday sooner rather than later, China's two competing exchanges will merge into one national exchange so that China's investors can speak with one voice. While the number of companies listed on the Shanghai Stock Exchange continues to grow, the Shenzhen Stock Exchange seems to have lost its appeal to companies since 2000. Back in 2000, Shanghai's mayor and many others promised the two exchanges would soon merge, but it never happened. A second board for emerging companies, a kind of mini-NASDAQ, is supposed to be added to Shenzhen operations. Technology being what it is, one big computerized board seems in the offing. It's turned out that way in many other countries: Australia had seven exchanges for more than one hundred years until consolidating into one, Hong Kong had four exchanges from 1969 to 1986. Europe is also in the process of further concentration due to the emergence of the euro as unified currency.

When I first came to China in 1984, there were still two currencies in use—the non-exchangeable renminbi (people's money) and the FEC (foreign exchange currency), for outsiders needing to buy items at special stores that ordinary Chinese couldn't access. Now that all seems like ancient history. Even until recently, they had separate and sometimes outlandish admission prices everywhere for foreigners. A lot of that has disappeared now because the difference in revenue just isn't worth the bother. Undoubtedly, this two-tiered approach to investing will prove equally cumbersome and unnecessary, and hopefully just as quickly. Besides, the system was put in place to discourage foreigners from speculation. But Chinese investors have a much higher rate of turnover (500 percent per year for A-shares versus 200 per year for B-shares), selling shares far more quickly.

All this may go hand in hand with the final hurdle: the full floating of the renminbi. The main thing that has to happen is that China's currency has to become freely convertible, so that relative values are clear and funds are easily transferred. How do I know this would be beneficial to the stock market? After the Chinese government announced its 2 percent appreciation of the renminbi on July 21, 2005, the Shanghai A-share index increased by 15 percent and the B-share index shot up an astonishing 25 percent.

Some experts contend that the renminbi has been undervalued by 15 percent or more. So far, the Chinese government has allowed a controlled float of nearly 7 percent by the start of 2007, not enough but far more than could have been expected just a few years back. Even if its currency doubled in value against the U.S. dollar, China would still have a trade surplus with the United States. The Japanese yen rose 400 percent against the dollar over several decades, yet Japan still has a trade surplus with the United States.

But a restricted float is only the first step in the Chinese government's move toward a free exchange of currency. Eventually, this would have a positive impact on the share prices of Chinese companies because corporate profits are in renminbi, and the renminbi would be worth more as compared to other currencies (as would the company's shares) . Naturally, the price of raw materials, which the companies import priced in dollars, will decrease. That will also boost profits.

While the United States often accuses China of purposefully maintaining low exchange rates in order to encourage exports (thus contributing to America's widening trade deficit), it is unlikely that China would do so at the expense of its own well-being. And artificially low rates encourage excess foreign currency inflow, which then causes speculative bubbles.

The real estate bubble is a prime example. If money can't appreciate or freely go where it likes, then property has to serve the purpose, and speculators have driven prices of real estate way too high for the Chinese in major cities such as Beijing, Shanghai, and Shenzhen. And so long as the renminbi is undervalued, this remains a tempting market for foreigners. In May 2006, *The Wall Street Journal* reported that the price of an average apartment in Beijing was thirteen times the annual average salary of its local residents.

However, China's leaders have been afraid to let their currency fully float, presuming that its citizens would move money out of the country and the renminbi would collapse. Another fear is that a higher rate of exchange would slow foreign investment. Needless to say, these fears are rooted in the mind-set of China's old guard.

While there might be some temporary effects to total convertibility, the market would soon find its proper level, just as it has with euros and dollars. Looking back at the period of appreciation of the Japanese yen in the latter half of the 1980s, the Japanese stock market experienced a tremendous surge in liquidity, driving up property markets and stock prices. This also led to an expansion of foreign investment by Japanese companies, including new production bases in the United States and in Southeast Asia to combat rising manufacturing costs. Japanese firms embarked on a wave of large-scale acquisitions of office buildings, hotels, and other overseas properties, all of which served to enlarge Japan's trade surplus. Similarly, China, by unpegging its currency, will allow itself to become a global player in business as never before. Besides, a country that will host the Olympics in 2008 and the Shanghai World's Fair in 2010 does not need a blocked currency.

These days, U.S. officials, Chinese stock regulators, and high government economists all seem to be speaking with the same voice. Everybody wants more mutual funds, index funds, and institutional investment. It looks like a true futures index, discussed fitfully for years, will finally be coming online. China's corporate bond market is also still very weak. Only 10 percent of China's firms use these types of self-financing—and these are made extremely difficult by long waiting periods—compared with 80 percent turning to corporate bond financing in the United States. In 2005, the total capital raised from corporate bonds in America was 6.5 times the amount raised in the stock market. By contrast, the amount raised through corporate bonds in China a year later was less than half the value of shares in the stock market.

There is also open discussion of proposals to abolish a maximum daily limit on price fluctuation—another sign of a more mature market. The clear trend is toward more options for investors and more direct access. In general, where there have been tensions between a centralized leadership in China and a decentralized economic system, the tensions have been resolved in favor of increasing prosperity and increasing openness. In fact, I've met plenty of businessmen who tell me they'd rather operate in China—which doesn't penalize or tax enterprise the way the United States and many Western countries do— than in any of the "free market" countries.

Over the long term, all reforms in the exchanges and the currency will positively affect stock prices. And one of these days, buying stocks of Chinese companies will be just as easy as calling your broker or clicking your mouse to place a trade in London and Frankfurt. I doubt that day will be long in coming.

2

Risk: The Perils of Success

In Chinese, the word "crisis" is made up of a combination of two characters. The first signifies "risk." The second stands for "opportunity."

China could face many crises up ahead. As an investor, the ones I need to examine most closely are those where potential risks—the fears they provoke, the solutions they require—have the best chance of creating value.

Believe it or not, I don't like taking chances when it comes to investing. The thrill of living on the edge has never been part of my portfolio. The same holds true for buying stocks in China, even if its people are among the biggest gamblers on earth. If you do your homework, buy cheap, and remain patient, you should be able to walk over and pick up that pile of cash in the corner that nobody else notices.

By today's accepted standards, China is a relatively safe place to invest. The PRS (Political Risk Services) Group, a leading organization in investment risk analysis, has ranked China as a "low risk" country since 2001. In 2006, using factors such as total foreign debt as a percentage of GDP, debt as a percentage of export goods and services, and international liquidity and exchange rate stability, China scored 47.5 on a scale of 50. Japan scored 46, the United States a lowly 30.5. In fact, the United States has been considered more risky than China since 2001—and that was before the September 11 attacks.

Still, nothing is certain when you are weathering downsides or exploiting upsides in markets. So assessing threats and anticipating pitfalls is essential—especially when you are looking halfway around the world. And there are about as many ways for things to go wrong in China as there are people.

Any unflinching list of danger points would have to include the following: potential military conflicts (especially with Taiwan); political instability (should the Communist Party lose or fritter away its legitimacy); separatists movements (in the Muslim Far West or in Tibet); general social unrest (among disaffected youth, wronged peasants or an increasingly democratic-minded middle class); widening gaps between rich and poor, or country and city (a recurrent theme in many of my chapters); labor turmoil (given the lack of union representation); dwindling resources (starting with water and oil); environmental threats (pollution, desertification); lurking epidemics (AIDS, SARS, bird flu); earthquakes (actual or financial) wreaking havoc on constructs without safe foundations (again, actual or financial); faulty and corrupt management practices and the larger costs of unchecked corruption in general; the growing influence of criminal syndicates; insider double-dealing and abuse; the potential collapse of the banking system due to bad loans or the collapse of the social security system due to the burdens of an aging population with fewer children; investment bubbles, frenzies, and crashes; a loss of competitive advantage as wages rise; bungled currency policy and overprotectionism; too much or too little foreign capital in play; leadership arrogance and incompetence; rising nationalism; and a lack of innovative thinking.

Sound familiar? Many of these risks occur everywhere, including the United States. There's plenty there to stay up nights worrying about, even if you're not a vice premier or party general secretary. But there's no need to calculate the odds for all of these risks.

Ultimately, China doesn't have to be perfectly mistake-free in order to produce some of the most profitable companies in the world. Its population doesn't have to reach American per capita income levels to rally commodities and product markets. Even if China's economy should grow only at 3 to 4 percent per year—sounds downright skimpy, doesn't it?—that would present many chances for growth. Most countries' finance ministers would sell their relatives for a 5 percent economic growth for their countries, a disappointing number for China. No one can expect 10 percent growth per annum for eternity.

Naturally, China is bound to face setbacks, sudden and gradual. Astute investors will get their confidence tested by periodic hurdles and occasional threats. So I've identified several major challenges that could pose the greatest risk to China's progress—and that will, in my estimation, present the most chances for investment upsides.

Flash Points and Talking Points

Pundits have been predicting "the coming war with China" since the day Bob Hope did his first TV special from the Great Wall. Some Cold War mind-sets still haven't thawed. The myth of "red Chinese aggression" seems to get brought out of mothballs whenever there's a point of contention (like the bombing of the Chinese embassy during the war in Serbia, which very few I met on my travels believed was an accident). Still, there's hardly been a ripple since China and the United States became overnight allies in the war against Islam-inspired terror—a conflict none of those pop prophets of doom ever saw coming.

Would China really bring out its guns to secure Central Asian oil? To defend other supply lines to vital resources? Or would it get pushed into conflict by a fading American empire turning to military force when all else has failed? One argument goes that emerging superpowers have always grown by flexing their newfound muscle, and swift economic growth provokes imperial ambitions. By the same token, countries that are doing as well as China has done at raising its own standard of living may not have to distract their people with foreign adventures.

China needs war like a hole in the head. Over the past hundred years, the place has been pillaged by foreign powers, plundered by feuding warlords, ravaged by decades of civil war, then punished by Japanese invasion, its major cities and industries raped and flattened. Americans tend to think of the Second World War as our moment of glorious sacrifice to save the world. The United States suffered over four hundred thousand casualties in that war, none of them civilian. China lost thirty-five million, second only to the Soviet Union, mostly innocent noncombatants. Property damage in China amounted to fifty times the GDP of Japan at that time. And we forget that the Chinese army was involved in the carnage of Korea, too (where Mao Zedong lost his only son).

A careful look at China's consistent behavior provides further reassurance. China is a vast, ethnically diverse and inward-looking country. It has always been too busy with domestic strife—born of competing fiefdoms, nationalities, or petty tyrants—to look for trouble elsewhere. While the Han majority has conquered neighbors to consolidate the territory that they consider "Chinese," their armies have hardly ever marched beyond the confines of their own Middle Kingdom. Why bother, when you already think you live in the middle of the world? Chinese explorer Cheng Ho set sail on ships twice the size of Columbus's ships in the fifteenth century and explored much of the world. Yet he never once annexed territory. Today, the current one-child policy, though slowly being amended, helps to underscore China's traditionally quietist attitude. Would today's Chinese families readily send their only children and grandchildren to war knowing they can never have more?

The Chinese invented gunpowder centuries before the Europeans. Yet instead of creating more terrifying weapons, they used it for fireworks. Their ships and navigational skills were better than those of the great European explorers, yet they never attempted to seize territory or set up colonies. Even though China has built up a modern nuclear arsenal, the cache is still relatively small, enough to raise the country's status and provide adequate deterrence, but not so much as to bankrupt the country's coffers or stage full-scale nuclear Armageddon. While exact numbers are secret, the Chinese government has claimed as recently as 2004 that it has the smallest arsenal of warheads of any major nuclear power (implying they have less than the United Kingdom's two hundred). The Pentagon estimates China has about forty intercontinental ballistic missiles (ICBM's), long- and short-range, accounting for the bulk of its nuclear strike force. China has begun deploying road- and sea-based missiles. They have also pledged publicly to a policy of "no first use" in general, and no strikes ever against nonnuclear nations. What is known for certain is that they have conducted only around 5 percent of the nuclear tests the United States or former Soviet Union have conducted.

Still, the Chinese government rattles its sabers a lot over the ongoing existence of that "other China," Taiwan. It's one issue they view as critical to their national sovereignty. But the more I've learned about the Taiwan situation, and the more I've traveled there, the more ambiguous the whole thing appears. Americans tend to view the conflict as a vestige of the civil war that the Kuomintang party lost to the Communists in 1949. However, it's now the old guard of the Kuomintang who most closely favor eventual reunification.

Others ignorant of local conditions may believe that U.S. meddling has propped up the "puppet" regime on a small tear-shaped island that still dares call itself the Republic of China. But, in keeping with the mainland's strict one-China policy, the United States cut off official ties with Taiwan in 1979. And since the lifting of martial law in 1987, Taiwan has become one of the most boisterous democracies in Asia—not so easy for the United States, or China, or even its own people, to control.

Very much under its own steam, Taiwan has gone on to become the fifth-largest economy in Asia—despite its small population of twenty-four million. Taiwan's GDP has grown at an average of 8 percent every year since the 1980s, as compared to 3 percent for the United States. In addition to being among the top five nations in terms of foreign currency reserves, Taiwan maintains a favorable balance of trade and is home to many of the world's biggest electronics manufacturers, including Inventec, Acer, and Quanta Corp., which supply computer components for companies such as HP, Dell, and Toshiba.

Taiwan's separate development from China—with an identity at once more Western and more traditionally Chinese in terms of values and religion—and its people's strongly anti-Communist training gave rise to a pro-independence movement in the 1990s that culminated in the election of Chen Shui-bian. He was not only the first native Taiwanese to rule the island but the first head of state in any Chinese society ever to take office through a peaceful transfer of power from one ruling party (Chiang Kai-shek's Nationalists) to another. But with his term coming to an end, China has already lived through its worst nightmare: a pro-independence president pushing openly for referenda and constitutional changes aimed at forever cementing the island's separate status. Just as Chen and his cohorts have been forced to lower their inflammatory rhetoric, so the Chinese government has shown again that its bark is far worse than its bite.

Both sides are wary of confrontation—and it's obvious why. Day by day, the economies of Taiwan and the mainland grow more interdependent. Nearly 50 percent of direct foreign investment to Taiwan came from China in 2005. Similarly, Taiwan is currently the second-largest contributor to China's inflow of foreign investment. Despite efforts to diversify, 63.3 percent of Taiwan's foreign investing goes to China, up 10 percent from 2005 to 2006. China has surpassed the United States to become Taiwan's biggest export market (21.6 percent of all exports in 2005). Bilateral trade exceeded US$100 billion in 2006, a 20 percent increase in a year.

Ever since the Taiwanese government lifted restrictions on Taiwanese investment in China, thousands of Taiwanese-owned companies have flooded the mainland to set up factories to take advantage of the mainland's lower production costs in telecom, clothing, and electronics. Taiwanese businessmen are moving to the mainland in droves—an estimated 750,000 by 2006—and taking capital with them. Despite remaining bureaucratic hurdles, 213 of Taiwan's 250 major corporations have already invested in China, according to a survey by the China Credit Institute.

These powerful business leaders are the first force pushing for a peaceful resolution to the Taiwan-China conflict. They know better than anyone that poor relations with the mainland have only prevented Taiwan from reaching its full potential. The obvious example is that there are no direct flights yet between the two Chinas, so a Taipei salesman trying to strike a deal in Shanghai—only 337 air miles away—has to go on an all-day journey through Hong Kong. Education is another area where close symbiosis could be readily achieved if and when the two sides ever make up. Taiwan has so many universities that many remain under-enrolled. Yet only 5.3 million students in China, 20 percent of those qualified to attend higher education, ever get the chance. Many of the others might be willing to pay good money for advanced studies in their own language on Taiwan.

Partners around Asia also have a lot to gain from a peaceful resolution to the Taiwan-China conflict. As China becomes richer, it is not only a better factory, providing neighbors with higher-quality goods at low prices, but also a better customer, offering neighbors more export income. Even Japan, China's historical adversary, is increasingly dependent on sales to China. Its exports to China rose five times between 1999 and 2003; in the first month of 2007, exports, many of them semiconductors, were up 50 percent over the previous year. Indeed, China has already replaced the United States as Japan's main trading partner. Like a modern-day sword of Damocles, the threat of China-imposed economic sanctions dangles over Japan. China is both South Korea's and North Korea's largest export market as well. Dependent on China for sustained growth and prosperity, these countries will continue to apply direct pressure for a peaceful resolution of the China-Taiwan conflict.

This doesn't mean there won't ever be a shot fired over Taiwan. Politicians have done dumber things. The bigger question is: how can one spot investment opportunities others may have missed due to unrealistic fears of a conflagration? Investing in Taiwanese companies that are themselves heavily involved in China may seem like a counterintuitive way to go. But corporate profits should increase as scores of Taiwanese companies move factories and offices to the mainland.

The Taiwanese manage some of the most technologically advanced electronics companies in the world, and although this sector faces intense competition, some quality companies stand to gain both in terms of the booming market in China and in terms of saving on labor costs.

Another strategy might be to invest in the province of Fujian, on the mainland just across from Taiwan. Most of Taiwan's original settlers came from Fujian and speak the local Fuzhou dialect. As a result of the ongoing tensions, real estate and other sectors are cheaper in Fujian compared to other developed regions of China. If real peace comes, Fujian is sure to boom. Its capital, Fuzhou, has seven million people, while Xiamen, in southern Fujian and with about two million people, is a thriving port that has recently been named as one through which China will ship its auto exports. The Fujianese, or Hokkien as they have been traditionally called, have always been willing, even eager, to ship out of China. Many have created successful businesses and communities throughout Southeast Asia, America, and now Europe, too. If a permanent peace with Taiwan is made, many could return to their home province with a wealth of expertise and capital.

You can also invest in the tourism sector, which I cover in a later chapter. Taiwan is, after all, China's largest island and lies to its southeast. It possesses mountain sanctuaries, gorges, temples, and beaches, and the island would be a popular destination for mainlanders if travel restrictions were eased.

Of course, if you want to act on the basis of pessimism in terms of the Taiwan problem, strategies are available, too. You can sell short Taiwanese companies that rely on the mainland for future growth—betting that if tensions escalate, resulting embargoes and sanctions will hurt profitability. Or you can invest in defense companies on either side, since they would undoubtedly thrive in times of conflict. In the worst case, you could simply wait to pick up bargains in the period of recession and recovery that follows a war. But you might be waiting for a long time. And if the United States or Japan gets drawn in, as they are committed to defending Taiwan, you might just be looking at World War III, in which case I'd suggest stocking up on all kinds of commodities. But not even the world's best broker could safeguard your portfolio in such an event.

In general, the specter of war aids the flow of capital to defense contractors, no matter where they are found. With reservists and police included, China's total military force numbers 3.2 million people—a serious crowd, but that's true for everything in China. The country is seeking to modernize its huge but often poorly equipped military forces by building or purchasing new ships, missiles, and fighter planes. For 2007, China's official budget for military spending rose 17.8 percent—the most ever—now representing slightly more than 7 percent of the national budget (relatively low compared to the U.S. percentage), but marking the eighteenth consecutive year of double-digit growth.

The U.S. Pentagon believes that this budget doesn't include new weapons systems—China imports about US$3 billion worth from Russia every year—nor its missiles nor research. So the actual budget could be three times what's stated, perhaps somewhere over US$100 billion for 2007. At the same time, China buys hardware and systems from many European firms, which will have the most to gain, since U.S. laws prevent such sales by American firms.

All this makes American hard-liners very nervous. But my faith is in the cold economics (if not the warm-blooded mammals). We've all heard about the so-called McDonald's factor. No two countries that serve up Big Macs have ever taken up arms against each other. In this case, I'd call it a pax cemented by Chinese dumplings. Given China's vast labor force and markets, and Taiwan's expertise and capital, the two would make a perfect fit. Maybe one of these days, even the Chinese themselves will be calling it a match made in heaven.

Jim's Sino Files: First in War, First in Peace

Note: For all companies, exchange locations are followed by ticker symbols, which may be numbers only, numbers and letters, or letters only.

China Aerospace International Holdings
HKG (Hong Kong exchange): 0031, H-shares; OTC: CAIF
Three-year trend: profits US$15.1 million up from US$17.7 million loss,
revenues up 40.5 percent

Military budgets are forecast to rise in double digits for at least the next five years. And plenty of companies will benefit from this ongoing spending spree by and for the People's Liberation Army. But most of the Chinese defense industry is comprised of eleven state-owned enterprises that are not publicly traded—except for subsidiaries of China Aerospace International Holdings that are engaged in missile research, development, and production.

Jiangxi Hongdu Aviation Industry Co., Ltd.
SHA (Shanghai exchange): 600316, A-shares
Three-year trend: profits up 108.1 percent, revenues down 10 percent

China's defense budget is far from transparent. So defense stocks tend to be murky as well, a fertile ground for all sorts of market rumors. And defense companies are waived from having to disclose military-related information, making forecasts of their sales and profits even tougher. Hongdu Aviation is the only manufacturer of training aircraft in China. Its products include the K8 jet trainer, which is exported to many countries, such as Pakistan, Sri Lanka, Zambia, and Egypt. The latest trainer model, the L15, made its maiden flight in 2007. Hongdu has also embarked on civil aircraft building, as part of a consortium of Chinese companies and institutions that have partnered with Airbus on a US$633 million aircraft assembly plant in Tianjin.

Jiangnan Heavy Industry Co., Ltd.
SHA: 600072, A-shares
Three-year trend: profits up 78.4 percent, revenues up 58.7 percent

Jiangnan is one of a consortium of companies that will help build China's first aircraft carrier. When rumor was circulated that it was moving its plant from its old site near the Bund to Changxing Island, share prices skyrocketed threefold in less than two months at the end of 2006.

Sichuan Chengfa Aero Science & Technology Co., Ltd.
SHA: 600391, A-shares
Three-year trend: profits up 89.6 percent, revenues up 88.7 percent

This is the largest manufacturer of fighter aircraft engines and parts in China—a supplier to General Electric and Rolls-Royce. Exports account for 65 percent of revenue, but the company expects lower domestic sales in 2007.

With China announcing plans to build its own civilian jumbo jets eventually, competing against Boeing and Airbus, the growth in travel alone should also boost the domestic aerospace industry.

Xiamen ITG Group Corp., Ltd.
SHA: 600755, A-shares
Three-year trend: profits up 65.8 percent, revenues up 47.5 percent

On a more peaceful note, this company specializes in trade between Taiwan and Xiamen Special Economic Zone. It handles agriculture products, medical equipment, and many other goods and commodities and indirectly owns 15.3 percent of shares in Xiamen International Container Terminals, the only pier that can accommodate current-generation container ships at Fujian's port of Xiamen, the nearest major Chinese port to Taiwan. If any company should profit from better relations between the "two Chinas," this is it.

Fujian Expressway Development Co., Ltd.
SHA: 600033, A-shares
Three-year trend: profits up 23.7 percent, revenues up 25.3 percent

Would be another indirect beneficiary of better bilateral relations. The company operates two superhighways: from the coastal city of Qianzhou to the provincial capital of Fuzhou, and from Fuzhou to

Xiamen. With a more solid peace across the Taiwan Strait, the volume of goods moving along these routes would increase dramatically. In addition, the two highways are main thoroughfares linking the booming Yangtze River Delta and Pearl River Delta.

Fujian Zhangzhou Development Co., Ltd.
SHE (Shenzhen exchange): 000753, A-shares
Three-year trend: profits down 54.5 percent, revenues up 28.4 percent

Many Taiwanese trace their heritage to the port city of Zhangzhou, making this a hot destination for investment by Taiwanese companies. Formosa Plastics invested US$3 billion in a power plant there. Fujian Zhangzhou Development is active there in road building, infrastructure development, and construction.

Formosa Plastics Corporation
TPE (Taipei exchange): 1301
Three-year trend: profits down 15 percent, revenues up 21 percent

One of the top three Taiwanese investors in China by volume. Tycoon Wang Yongqing, owner of FPC, has been investing in the mainland since his first trip there in 1990. Petrochemicals are the main focus. Founded in 1954, FPC is the largest producer of PVC resins in the world, with plants in the United States as well as Taiwan. In China, it has also branched into health care and power generating. The Taiwanese government objected to Wang's 1996 plan to build a power-generating plant in Fujian, but he restarted the project with local partners in 2003.

Uni-President Enterprises Corporation
TPE: 1216
Three-year trend: profits up 38.1 percent, revenues up 1.2 percent

Uni-President has branched out from family farms in Tainan, southern Taiwan, to become not just the largest food manufacturer on the island but one of the largest in Asia. It has been investing heavily in the mainland since 2002, known for its soft drinks and especially instant noodles—with eleven assembly lines churning out the popular snacks. Having expanded into convenience stores, oil, frozen food, and more, its mainland revenues were US$1.4 billion for 2005, and its stocks rose 15 percent the week it was chosen as a sponsor for the Beijing Olympics.

Foxconn International Holdings Ltd.

HKG: 2038, H-shares; OTC: FXCNF

Three-year trend: profits up 296 percent, revenues up 213.8 percent

Since Taiwanese companies are restricted to investing 40 percent of their assets in China, some have started spinning off mainland operations and listing them on Hong Kong exchanges. Foxconn is a main supplier of mobile handsets for Nokia and Motorola. Foxconn Group, which holds 74 percent of the shares of Foxconn International, announced in early 2007 a plan for eleven new projects on the mainland, to help ensure 30 percent growth for its computer and consumer electronics assembly and design divisions. Foxconn is part of Hon Hai Precision Ltd. (TPE: 2317; OTC: HNHAF, HNHPF), holder of fifteen thousand patents in various forms of computer assembly and technology, which announced in March 2007 that they will have eight big new projects throughout the mainland.

A Thirst for Progress

"We have seen the enemy and it is ourselves." That dictum, made popular by the comic strip Pogo during the Vietnam War, can apply to many countries around the world—especially China. It is internal problems, not external threats, that pose the greatest danger to China's prosperity.

Somewhere down the road, China's productivity will be limited by the resources it uses. Titanium, iron ore, copper, are not infinite. With its heavy reliance on coal, China is passing the United States as the world's worst emitter of greenhouse gases. This affects the whole planet: American authorities estimate that one quarter of all the particulate matter in the air above smoggy California now comes from China. Two thirds of China's cities have substandard air; sixteen of the twenty most-polluted cities on earth are found there. Approximately 80 percent of China's children in industrial areas have some form of lead poisoning.

Meanwhile, good land is being depleted by chemical saturation, and forests are being turned to desert—between 1994 and 1999 alone, the Gobi Desert extended by twenty thousand square miles and creeps closer to Beijing all the time. With half of the country's twenty-one thousand chemical companies situated near the Yangtze or Yellow rivers, incidents of toxic spills and poisoning are on the increase—there were forty-five in the last two months of 2005 alone. Seventy of China's main rivers and lakes are considered dangerously polluted.

When I consider China's future, I worry most about the place going dry. And I don't mean prohibiting moonshine. I mean serious water depletion. The prospects for India, by the way, could be even worse. In my travels through both countries, I came across numerous former cities of splendor turned to ghost towns for lack of water. Now history could repeat itself on a much grander scale. For starters, rainfall in the north of China, which hosts two thirds of the country's farmland, is less than 8 percent of the world average. The more tropical south, which provides the irrigation for 70 percent of the nation's grain, has fallen victim to rapid urbanization. The mighty Yangtze may be biologically dead by 2012: it now absorbs 40 percent of China's wastewater, 80 percent of which is untreated. Meanwhile, many treatment plants, like those on the giant Three Gorges Dam, are not being used to capacity. One hundred eighty cities depend on the Yangtze River for their drinking water, including Shanghai, Wuhan, and Chongqing, with a combined population of nearly sixty million. The cities keep going farther upstream to find better water, but one day, they will have nowhere to go.

Under Communism, water was viewed as a free resource of the people and prices were kept artificially low. Prices have risen steeply in recent years—ten times in the five years from 1999 to 2004—but that hasn't stemmed use. Even "green" initiatives could just make matters worse. Water specialists have warned that the growing trend toward biofuels like gasohol, gaining fashion in Brazil and India, may actually lead to an enormous increase in the amount of water needed to grow sugar as a fuel crop.

As a result, China has been designated by the United Nations as among the world's lowest thirteen countries in terms of water per capita. By 2030, the country's own Ministry of Water Resources predicts such resources will fall 20 percent lower, to a mark coinciding with internationally recognized levels of "water stress." Over 60 percent of China's 660 cites are already running short. And half the country's populace drinks water contaminated with levels of human and animal waste that exceed national and international standards. The World Bank believes water pollution is costing from 1 to 12 percent of the GDP in disaster relief and health problems.

The Chinese aren't just turning to Perrier. Since 2000, the government has started imposing a series of environmental standards and mandates on Chinese companies and municipalities, and it has set water use restrictions on five key industries, including petrochemicals, textiles, and paper. The Ministry of Water Resources expects to spend one trillion renminbi, or US$125 billion, by 2010 to rescue the national water system. These figures include 330 billion renminbi, or US$41.25 billion, to construct urban wastewater treatment facilities and 320 billion renminbi, or US$40 billion, for two main lines of the south-to-north water diversion project.

If the Chinese become desperate enough, they will turn to neighboring Russia for water, as they have for oil. I'll never forget my own motorcycle ride along the shores of Lake Baikal in Siberia. The deep reserves of this lake, the largest freshwater lake anywhere, contain over 20 percent of the world's freshwater, more than all of North America's Great Lakes combined. Interestingly enough, Lake Baikal once belonged to the Chinese empire. There is a lot of water in Siberia and few people, but it may take years to divert the water to the South.

China has begun to admit publicly that it does not have the expertise to manage such issues, and is privatizing and opening up the water sector to foreign investment. The government has finally admitted the social costs as well. Well aware that the effects of pollution are costing the country up to 10 percent of GDP, or US$200 billion each year, the government has just made a commitment of US$162 billion over the next five years to aid in the cleanup. A slew of new regulations have been passed: to encourage alternative forms of energy, to battle desertification and the poisoning of rivers, to create a new generation of water treatment facilities, and to enforce environmental laws more strictly (China's State Environmental Protection Administration, until recently, had only a token staff of three hundred).

Traditionally, the bulk of foreign funding for water facilities in China came from the World Bank, the Asian Development Bank, and foreign government donations. To address funding issues, the Chinese government has started actively encouraging the private sector to purchase existing or newly built wastewater treatment plants at below replacement cost. According to the U.S. Department of Commerce, there are currently three hundred institutions, foreign and domestic, engaged in water supply research and engineering design, wastewater collection, and wastewater treatment in China. Several hundred factories produce wastewater treatment equipment materials. However, companies with a good balance sheet, technological capability, and Chinese support will prosper from China's water opportunity.

Managing water resources may be the world's central crisis of the coming century. As such, China won't be alone in looking for solutions. But unless it finds them, the country's golden age could be cut off at the tap.

Jim's Sino Files: Liquid Profits

Bio-Treat Technology Ltd.
SIN (Singapore exchange): B22, S-shares
Three-year trend: profits down 9.5 percent, revenues up 133.7 percent

Some of the biggest beneficiaries of China's water crisis will be found in the Chinese-run enclave of Singapore, where treatment companies have advanced technologies, a keen understanding of the Chinese business environment, and good connections with China's government. Singapore's government is already aiming to capture 3 to 5 percent of the estimated global water treatment market, projected to be worth US$1.2 trillion within ten years.

On reclaimed marshland itself, Singapore has the expertise and funding to become the Silicon Valley of water treatment, if you will. The Singapore stock exchange reflects this ambition, hosting a majority of Asia's one hundred water treatment stocks, valued at US$50 billion. Bio-Treat has implemented 250 wastewater treatment systems in China and is contracted to work on China's massive south-to-north water diversion project.

Asia Environment Holdings Ltd.
SIN: A58, S-shares
Three-year trend: profits up 287.3 percent, revenues up 209.1 percent

Signed large deals with Jiangsu and Jiangxi provinces. Shared with two main Singapore water firms in China contracts worth US$474 million.

Other Singapore firms **Hyflux (SIN: 600; OTC: HYFXF; profits down 35.1 percent, revenues up 46.5 percent)** and **Sinomem (SIN: S14; OTC: SMMKF; profits up 23.2 percent, revenues up 111 percent)** operate in the filtration process. Hyflux has ventured into the treatment of the liquid produced from the decomposition of garbage in landfills.

Asia Water Technology Ltd.
SIN: 5GB, S-shares
Three-year trend: profits up 121.9 percent, revenues up 46.5 percent

Asia Water has seen nice share price increases and has over five hundred projects in China.

China Water Affairs Group Ltd.
HKG: 0855, H-shares; OTC: CWAFF
Three-year trend: US$3.2 million loss up from US$12.6 million loss, revenues up 59.4 percent

Mixes water utilities with aquaculture and electronics.

Shanghai Young Sun Investment Co., Ltd.

SHA: 900935, B-shares

Three-year trend: profits up 25.4 percent, revenues up 107.2 percent

A local Chinese sewage treatment specialist that is expanding.

Nalco Company

NYSE (New York Stock Exchange): NLC

Three-year trend: profits up 76.3 percent, revenues up 6.3 percent

Many multinationals are looking for opportunities in China and other crisis areas around the world. Nalco is a water treatment company in Illinois that recently announced it has stepped up sales efforts in emerging economies.

Veolia Environnement

EPA (Euronext Paris): VIE; NYSE: VE, ADR; OTC: VEOEF

Three-year trend: profits up 76.3 percent, revenues up 6.3 percent

French firm that owns utilities in China providing water and sewer services to 110 million people.

Among other foreign companies, Siemens (NYSE: SI) recently joined forces with Mekerot, Israel's biggest water utility, not publicly traded, to explore new technologies to reuse scarce water in Israel, and to ultimately sell it to nations such as China. In July 2006, Dow Chemical (NYSE: DOW) bought Zhejiang Omex Environmental Engineering, a Chinese company that adds three more water purification technologies to Dow's portfolio.

Fujian Longking Co., Ltd.

SHA: 600388, A-shares

Three-year trend: profits down 69.7 percent, revenues up 53.9 percent

There are going to be more and more so-called green companies in China, looking to clean up through cleaning up the country. Founded in 1998, Fujian Longking is the first listed company in China that produces machinery for desulfurization and dust cleaning. It has worked with German affiliates to introduce numerous environmental protection technologies.

Zhejiang Feida Environmental Science & Technology Co., Ltd.
SHA: 600526, A-shares
Three-year trend: profits down 57.7 percent, revenues up 41.7 percent

Started in 2002, Zhejiang Feida specializes in incinerators and filters aimed at air pollution—an area with plenty of work ahead.

When All Else Fails, Will China?

Every book that comes out about China seems to suggest that the country is right at its tipping point. It's dramatic to say and most convenient for selling lots of copies. But when I look at China, I don't see a country about to conquer the world or plunge into chaos. In case you haven't figured it out by now, I see a continuum. And I take the long view, just like China's leaders and patient negotiators tend to do.

In the last thirty years, China has managed to pull off nothing less than a social revolution—with a minimum of bloodshed and strife and with maximum return. Huge relocations of population and reallocations of funds and resources have come off without mass victimization, mass unrest, or even runaway inflation. The people who have managed that change—like China's first economic czar, Zhu Rongji, who once wowed Harvard Business School students with his knowledge of Wall Street terminology—showed incredible savvy and street smarts. And the people following them are even more technocrats, trained in the West and familiar with every wrinkle of the modern capitalist state and business formation.

These people seem to know when to keep the lid tight and when to let the lid off to let out social steam—and there is a lot of that. In 2005, for instance, it was estimated that there were 510,000 "public disputes" across China. This isn't necessarily a bad thing, but a sign that some forms of protest are being allowed. Of course, no one looks to the massacre of students at Tiananmen Square as a brilliant example of policing, but to most Chinese, that response and the tensions between old and new guards are distant history. Unlike the Japanese, who the Chinese themselves view as moving in lockstep, the Chinese have always tended to battle and express dissent among themselves. But will such turmoil under heaven rise to the point where it would seriously affect the business and investment climate? Ask most Chinese today what they want, and they'll say, to make money and see their country have a prosperous and stable future. Most of the Chinese I've met are pulling strenuously in the same direction.

Even as China's economy expanded at 11 percent in 2006, *Barron's* magazine ran a cover story called "What Could Go Wrong With China?" The article's author pointed to three serious problems for China: an aging populace, widespread corruption, and environmental degradation. But he missed more obvious trends: hundreds of millions of rural dwellers able to replenish China's aging labor force for decades, similar levels of corruption in all of the so-called Asian Tigers not so long ago, and China's environmental problems presenting a huge opportunity for foreign and domestic companies.

And today, anyone who travels to Beijing can see, as the capital prepares for its green Olympics, that talk of cleaning up the environment has moved from a semidangerous cause espoused by a few dissidents to the main government thrust and the most covered cause in the state-run media. China's premier, Wen Jiabao, has exhorted his countrymen to move more quickly on this issue and has appointed not one but two ministers for the environment. It took the United States over a hundred years to face what "progress" had done to the North American continent; China may not succeed for a long time, but it is facing up to its problems within scant years of creating them.

China will also have to be ever watchful for the specter of new viruses, breeding potential pandemics like the 2003 SARS scare. One thing we can be sure of as a result of that experience: China's public health officials won't be hiding the true extent of a disease just to "save face." One thing none of us can know for sure is whether China's Guangdong province, with its overcrowded population in close proximity to a variety of wild animals, including many they regularly eat, really is the engine for mutated viruses that some researchers claim. China already has its fair share of known pathogens in the populace: 110 million carriers of hepatitis B and C, and up to 500 million people who have latent in their bodies the bacteria that causes tuberculosis.

Then there's the notion that India will somehow jump into the fray and grab much of China's commerce and momentum. No doubt this new kid on the emerging nations block is showing signs that it wants to become a world economic power. But aside from China's more efficient planning and more educated workforce, China also has a twenty-five-year head start. On my road trips beyond India's elite big cities, I saw business, or lack of business, as usual: poverty, overpopulation, inertia, and lack of basic facilities.

Aside from its rigid caste system and an unchecked birthrate among those who can least afford it, India has been ambivalent at best toward entrepreneurship, capital, and deregulation. Even companies like Kentucky Fried Chicken and McDonald's have run into trouble by moving too fast. The country's mountains of red tape and convoluted legal procedures are enough to put off even the most motivated investors. According to the World Bank, it takes more than twice as long to start a business in India than in China, and almost twice as long to register property or to enforce a contract (425 days in India to 241 in China).

As for infrastructure, I know firsthand that a journey of one hundred miles can be a whole-day affair in India. There's still an obvious lack of dependable electrical plants and decent port facilities. Shanghai alone handled twenty-one million shipping containers in 2005; all of India handled five million. Indian factories suffer, on average, seventeen power failures a month. As for communication, tough enough given India's twenty main dialects, we had to change cell phones as we moved from state to state in India. And when it comes to an educated populace, China requires all its children to finish grade six; half of India's future workforce never make it that far.

Every day now, headlines tell us how China is building trade and diplomatic links to the rest of Asia, and to Africa and Latin America for the long haul. Having already gone through the worst of its enormous restructuring, the world's largest country, largest factory, and largest market is not just going to fold up its tent and go away.

In the meantime, the main pressing questions are those of scale and pace. Will China float its currency freely enough? The answer already seems to be yes, as levels against the dollar are increasingly relaxed. And will that higher value put a crimp in exports? How will the banking system respond to a far greater foreign presence due to WTO-enforced openings? Can the necessary reforms in investment and stock regulations come fast enough? And what if the Western economies suffer enough of a serious slowdown that the orders to all those busy Chinese factories stop coming?

Folks in finance have a way of making it seem as though the world may come to an end after the next Federal Reserve bank meeting. Some analysts think that the U.S. economy is headed toward rough waters, with a housing slowdown, vast debt, and trade imbalances dragging down prices, income, and economic growth. Some also argue that China itself is headed for a "hard landing" as the government struggles to control growth.

While China's growth is dependent on the United States to some extent, the tie may not be as strong as you may think. China's stock market has periodically demonstrated itself to be a buffer during times of high volatility in U.S. stocks. China's market soared 38 percent during the Asian financial crisis in 1997. More recently, in 2000, the market surged forward with a 49 percent gain even as global markets faltered under the collapse of the Internet bubble. Recent blips show that the two markets are getting more linked, as more individual and especially institutional investors are getting the message and paying attention to happenings on the other side of the other big pond. But it's still mainly a psychological effect on confidence and growth. In real economic terms, the impact isn't as great as one might think. It's even lessening on a regional level, where China's Asian neighbors are busy developing on their own.

In Japan, the number of investors had grown to thirty million, or a quarter of the population, as of the end of 2000, from five million in September 1950 when the Nikkei 225 was introduced. In the United

States, fifty-three million households, just around half of American households, owned stocks and mutual funds in 2000, as reported by the Federal Reserve. In China, while the number of investment accounts has grown from nothing to sixty-five million in ten years, and is now growing at an amazing pace, it still represents 10 percent of the population.

The reality is that the United States is not the only influence in China, because much of China's growth has been internal and stimulated by domestic demand. Perceptions can influence markets. A lot of institutional investors have it in their heads that China is dependent on the United States in all regards. When something goes wrong in the United States, capital actually drains to the opposite side of the world, driving up China's prices and returns. Besides, we are the world's biggest debtor nation and China is the world's largest creditor. Maybe that should give you a clue about who to be concerned about the most.

When stocks drop even a fraction in the United States, it affects nearly everyone in terms of pensions, savings, property values, etc. That isn't true in China—not yet and not for a long while, even if 350,000 brokerage accounts are added in a month, as happened in January 2007, or if every rickshaw driver and village chieftain is playing the margins. China is a country with a very high savings rate and a very small fraction of people who are dependent on their stock portfolios. A stock crash wouldn't even have the same impact on capital for expansion. Without getting too technical, China's companies still have plenty of places other than the stock market where they can find funds, including a state with big pockets. Of course, manias can happen, buying and selling frenzies are part of the game, and we have to be wary of them. If things get bubbly enough, then you have to get out. But China is on a different growth trajectory than the United States, just as Japan and Germany were on different growth trajectories after the Second World War. Those trajectories can be slowed or sped up by outside events, but I don't believe that their basic shape will be altered.

Should China's rulers lose patience with "renegade" Taiwan, the myriad investors on that island or elsewhere vying for a way into China will not walk away. If bootleg software and pirate DVD's are still peddled on every Chinese street corner, foreign companies won't abandon the hundreds of millions of customers able to pay for legally protected goods. If tensions flare between China's haves and its have-nots or a mystery virus like SARS paralyzes production, the damage should be limited and temporary. And if manias for the market set off roller coasters, that would not necessarily affect a basic upward track. Everything points toward better management, less government zigzags in policy, more consistency, and more trust in the free flow of information.

It is China's success, of course, that poses the greatest challenge. "Excess liquidity, balooning credit, an asset boom and over-investment in loss-making heavy industries, all factors in Japan's downturn in the 1980's," have been cited as concerns by the Bank for International Settlements. Even China's top leaders have publicly described their nation's growth as "uncoordinated and unsustainable."

Overexuberance, bred by impatience and greed, is certainly the last but not least of the country's major concerns. Certainly, the boom that has gripped the stock market starting in 2005 has turned into an incipient bubble. In the very midst of writing this book, ordinary Chinese woke to the same truth about the value lodged in their stock markets that I have been trying to impart. And once you start reading about taxi drivers hocking their cabs to put their life savings into hot tips, or shop clerks borrowing from friends to make a quick play, that's the time to get cautious. Historically, there's no upside to hysteria. In addition, any downturn will be exacerbated by "back-office" problems—errors and delays caused by the sheer volume of all of those trades. Every mania market in history has led to problems and failures when the systems for accounts, payments, and transactions have become overwhelmed. So you might wait if China seems to be getting to a perilous stage. When there are corrections, then jump in. And if you can't buy when the market is depressed or discouraged, then at least look for solid investments that are rising steadily rather than shooting toward the heavens like Chinese-made firecrackers.

Whatever the risks, this much is clear: it's more scary to have all your savings in the U.S. stock market than it is to put a portion in China — whether investing in China's growth or as a hedge against a potential U.S. slowdown.

China is already a formidable financial market in its own right. There will be enormous opportunities there no matter what happens on the other side of the world. Astute investors will get their confidence tested by periodic hurdles and occasional clouds of crisis. If you are as convinced as I am of China's promise, you will invest when fear depresses prices, and benefit in the long term.

3

Companies: Let a
Thousand Brands Bloom

stock exchange is only as promising as the companies it lists. That's true in Shanghai or Frankfurt. My faith in China's markets stems from the country's numerous strong companies, which have only just begun realizing their limitless potential.

In China, the term "national champion" isn't used to refer just to winning sports teams. It's a label used by the government to boost and honor homegrown companies able to compete globally and to plant a Chinese logo overseas. It's like a Medal of Honor for entrepreneurship. By now, most people have heard of Haier, the world's fourth-largest producer of appliances; Tsingtao brewers (now partly owned by Anheuser-Busch); or Lenovo, the Chinese computer maker that acquired IBM's PC line. And Nanjing Automobile is starting to assemble the prestigious MG sports cars in China after snatching up England's Rover brand.

But those familiar firms are just the tip of a profit-making iceberg. From now on, it is China's rapidly expanding domestic demand that will drive earnings as well as price shares. A billion-plus people, it turns out, need a lot of companies to make and sell the components of a modern society, with ever-increasing efficiency, on a scale the world has never quite seen. That means the Chinese GE, the Chinese

Oracle, the Chinese Johnson & Johnson, the Chinese Sony are all out there somewhere, ready to be spotted. It could be just a matter of learning to read the packaging in Chinese.

Demanding New Brands

When you think groceries, you probably don't visualize LIANHUA on your bag, paper or plastic. But when it comes to crowding China's supermarket aisles, Lianhua bags more customers than its better-known foreign rivals Wal-Mart and Carrefour. Beginning with a single store in Shanghai, at last count Lianhua ran 3,716 all-purpose "hypermarts," groceries, and "Quik" convenience stores and are growing at four hundred new stores a year. Listed on the Hong Kong exchange since its IPO in 2003, the supermarket, owned in turn by the Bailian Group, China's largest overall retailer, now has consumers in their aisles in twenty-one provinces. (For the record, mainland China is divided into twenty-two provinces—though they count Taiwan as the twenty-third—plus four autonomous regions like Inner Mongolia, four municipalities, and the two special administrative regions of Hong Kong and Macau.)

With forty-seven thousand employees, Lianhu is working hard to stay ahead of its foreign competitors and is helping to standardize food supply chains. And it continues to win awards from retail associations as China's outstanding franchise brand. It has even begun opening its own outlets in Europe. And by the time of the Beijing Olympics, the company aims to have up to eight thousand outlets—in a country that as recently as 1999 had exactly one (I repeat, one) store defined as a supermarket.

Today, China's main enterprise is no longer just offering cut-rate goods to Western nations, but the country is rapidly getting up to speed at catering to its own consumers. According to U.S. Bureau of Labor Statistics estimates, China's labor force of eight hundred million people worked for an average of US$0.64 per hour in 2004—compared with US$21.11 for their U.S. counterparts. Since then, twenty-nine of the thirty-one provinces have raised their minimum wage. But the highest of these still works out to US$105 per month. Such wages will continue to give Chinese firms tremendous price advantage on the world scene. But booming demand and limited supply is already making unskilled labor more expensive in developed southern and eastern areas—causing businesses (including General Motors, Ford, Honda, Motorola, and Intel) to head farther west. And that means greater spending power for each segment of the populace as they move up the labor chain.

In the cities, wages and desires for a better life are rising fast. Urban white-collar workers are getting downright spoiled: most firms' biggest headache is keeping educated employees from jumping for better offers. Some analysts who define "middle class" by an annual per capita income of over US$1,200 in purchasing power parity argue that China already has a middle class of 470 million, more than the population of the United States. Others, with a stricter set of guidelines, put that number between 70 and 150 million, while the government itself says around 250 million, or 19 percent of the population, are in a position to afford a car, a condo, and more. But there's no doubt that this group's numbers are growing.

On the production side, two decades of expertise gained in joint ventures with foreign firms are helping Chinese enterprises leapfrog ahead of competitors. With outside companies eager to gain access to the world's largest market, local partners come away with increased manufacturing capacity and intellectual property. Keeping national expenditures on research and development low by international standards, the Chinese government has wisely encouraged foreign investment in some of its weakest sectors so domestic companies can benefit. Even in the past few years, as China has prepared for the tough foreign competition it must allow under WTO membership, four of China's five major banks have entered into strategic partnerships. And these banks have sold up to their limit of 20 percent ownership to experienced firms like Bank of America so that the banks can implement new management procedures. Now Chinese banks, too, are shedding their no-nonsense image and offering a far wider package of financial services. Sure, Volkswagen will profit in the short term in China's market, but Shanghai Automotive, its domestic ally, will be the long-term beneficiary.

China is moving away from fake purses and baby chairs, from traditional exports like textiles and toys to higher-value precision products like automotive parts. One index shows China's technology-intensive exports doubled in the decade from 1993 to 2004. Keep in mind what happened in Japan—still the model of development for all Asian economies (though few Chinese would give their old adversary such credit). Even into the early 1970s, products "Made in Japan" were ridiculed as cheesy, crude knockoffs. Remember those Godzilla monsters that looked like they were sewn together from rag dolls? It was all turned around by the same factors seen in China today: innovation combined with work ethic, high rates of saving, and large companies closely linked to government interests. But China is twenty-five times bigger than Japan and possesses the kind of hunger and initiative Japan may have lost.

The Haier Group, begun on a shoestring from a failing state enterprise and now the world's fourth-largest manufacturer of white goods, publicly rates the performance of each of its fifty thousand employees and literally makes the poorer ones stand in a corner. In a popular, propagandistic film about the company, the Communist militant is replaced as hero by the forward-thinking entrepreneur, in this case Haier's founder, the legendary Zhang Ruimin. The entrepreneur goes to Germany to study quality production, and then when his workers proudly produce their first batch of refrigerators, he makes them smash every one apart with hammers and build them again without defects.

Haier's problems now are how to manage their huge growth. In recent years, they've set up a half-dozen plants and a corporate presence in the United States, the Middle East, Africa, and Russia. Haier's overseas income from sales grew 51 percent in 2005, accounting for a record 31 percent of total revenue. But the company reported a downturn in profits in recent years, partly because of the price of overseas expansion—and fiercer domestic competition. Though they still take 30 percent market share at home, they, like every other large

Chinese corporation, can't afford to take their growing domestic market for granted.

Everywhere, Chinese CEO's are putting in long hours and maximum effort in a country where hard work is a religion and six-day weeks are the norm. They have the know-how and connections to produce more for less. They have studied well the lessons of start-ups and capital creation the world over—and their kids are out getting their MBA's. Today, all those factory managers trained in Western ways are branching out on their own and producing for their own.

Jim's Sino Files: Household Names in Hangzhou

China Life Insurance Co., Ltd.
SHA: 601628, A-shares; HKG: 2628, H-shares; NYSE: LFC, ADR; OTC: CILJF
Three-year trend: profits up 177.6 percent, revenues up 91.8 percent

A behemoth in a rapidly expanding field (30 percent annual growth since 1996). With the demise of the socialist system's "iron rice bowl," individual families now have to build their own safety nets. That's led to a huge, if not exactly unexpected, demand for all sorts of insurance, whether medical, life, or pension plans. In a market projected to soon exceed US$100 billion, three major players—China Life, China Ping An Insurance (cited later), and the much smaller China Pacific Insurance—rule the roost, with China Life and its seventy-six thousand employees holding down 43 percent of the market share at last count. And while Chinese banks face increasing competition from peer and foreign competitors who are allowed direct access to Chinese savers through WTO provisions, insurers face no such immediate threat (though domestic banks themselves may gradually offer more insurance services).

China Shenhua Energy Co., Ltd.
HKG: 1088, H-shares; OTC: CUAEF
Three-year trend: profits up 92 percent, revenues up 63.6 percent

China's growing power in the world is fed by a growing need for power (as in energy fuels). While many investors focus on oil companies, China still relies on coal to provide 70 percent of its electric output. Shenhua runs the best coal mine in China and does a lot more. It owns a railway linking mines in Shaanxi province and Inner Mongolia to its own company-owned seaport. Shenhua has also built power plants along its rail route—nine in all—and has invested US$1.58 billion in coal-to-oil conversion.

Shanghai Tyre and Rubber Co., Ltd.
SHA: 600623, A-shares; 900909, B-shares (listed as Double Coin Holdings);
OTC: SIRBY, SIRBF
Three-year trend: profits up 24.8 percent, revenues up 34.5 percent

Not as known as Goodyear, but having some very good years. The fifteenth-largest tire manufacturer in the world, Shanghai Tyre dominates domestic consumption with its Double Coin and Warrior brand names. It is becoming known internationally for heavy vehicle tires used on trucks and trailers. Formed in 1990 from an aggregate of state-owned monopolies, the company took off a decade later after the government categorized radial tires as a high-tech product exempt from certain taxes. Shanghai Tyre also went in on a joint venture with Michelin—but now the two are in fierce competition. As one Michelin executive has stated, "China will be the world battleground for tires."

Aluminum Corp. of China Ltd. (Chalco)
SHA: 601600, A-shares; HKG: 2600; NYSE: ACH, ADR
Three-year trend: profits up 86.7, revenues up 88.8 percent

The largest producer of primary aluminum in the world's fastest-growing aluminum market, and now the core of a group of ninety smaller aluminum-producing companies. Established in 1999 out of state-owned firms, Chalco has been slowed somewhat by lower prices due to increased production. There are reports that this number-two aluminum manufacturer in the world is planning aggressive acquisitions, including a possible takeover bid for Alcoa. While some new plants are being built, others in China have been closing due to high electricity costs. But world demand for this commodity continues to grow.

Huawei Technologies Co., Ltd.
Unlisted, Hong Kong IPO planned
Three-year trend: profits unavailable, revenues up 166.7 percent

Never heard of Huawei (pronounced "wha-way")? This privately owned giant in telecommunications equipment, founded by a former Chinese army officer, is a vendor in nearly one hundred countries, with a strong presence in the Middle East and research centers in India, Russia, Sweden, and the United States. Back in 2000, Cisco sued Huawei for patent infringement over telecom equipment. The two settled out of court. Now Huawei has evolved beyond mere copycat, and products are increasingly state-of-the-art, and the company claims 48 percent of its sixty-one-thousand-person workforce is involved in research and development.

Dynamic Dynasties

China's emergence on the world stage should hardly take anyone by surprise. If China's new companies are showing surprising confidence and drive, that may be due to their country's vast reservoir of experience in trade and invention. You could say that when it comes to business, no place on earth has a longer track record. For eternity, it seems, Chinese people have been driven by an abiding desire to make sure, as one key Chinese saying goes, "Each generation will be greater than the last."

Whenever I spend time with Chinese people, whether hotshot economists or humble vendors, I hear them referring constantly to models found in ancient courts, lessons learned from distant poets, and cautionary tales of military strategy stretching back through eons. Even as their country speeds into the future, China's past is very much alive. For much of that past, the Middle Kingdom, as China has called itself, was a center of innovation and commerce, among the most advanced civilizations.

Even in the sixteenth century, when European explorers took the lead by venturing to the New World, over half the silver found in the Americas ended up in China as payment for trade. Only the past two centuries have been an exception, fostering the image of China as the "sick man" of the East. Just as China's population through various periods has accounted for one third of humanity, China's economic position in the world has been right at the top for at least one third of humankind's chronology.

Like most visitors, the first time I glimpsed China's capacity for productive output was outside the ancient capital of Xi'an, at one time the largest city on earth, at the site of the so-called terra-cotta warriors. Here, tourists view over eight thousand life-size pottery figures of a vast army, spread over 160,000 square feet, all created over a span of thirty-eight years in the second century B.C. to help protect the first Qin emperor even in death. Talk about the world's first assembly line! A farmer stumbled upon this amazing find back in 1974, and parts of the mausoleum are still yet to be opened. Archaeologists continue to look for more. Like the Taj Mahal, no description or snapshot prepares you for human achievements with such a grand sweep. It's the same with China's history—and its potential.

Peking man casts a long shadow. China may not be the oldest civilization on earth but it has a decent claim to being the longest running. There are records of cultures along the Indus and the Nile that may predate those beside China's Yellow River, but evidence of rice cultivation and recognizably "Chinese" art reaches back around seven thousand years. Nobody can use hieroglyphics or speak Latin now, but China's written language evolved from that period and is still understood. But when Chinese claim theirs is a nation stretching back five thousand years, they may be overselling a bit. Most archaeologists date its continuity of kingdoms as stretching back just over four thousand.

At a time when Cleopatra struggled to maintain control of Egypt by securing a relationship with Julius Caesar, who would become the first emperor of Rome, China had long been unified under the Han Dynasty (206 B.C.–A.D. 220). And it traded widely with the West; Cleopatra herself treasured Chinese silk gowns. At their height, the Han and Roman empires conquered roughly the same amount of territory. But while the Romans ruled many distinct peoples, the Han—as the ethnic majority of Chinese would come to be known—ruled for four hundred years over a society that imposed a common writing system and adopted the practical morality-based teachings of a sage named Confucius as the basis for a just state.

While Europe was mired in its so-called Dark Ages, when science and classic learning were rejected in favor of narrow-minded theocracy, China continued to develop and innovate through three golden periods: Tang (618–907), Song (960–1279), and Yuan (1279–1368). You might say that when the Western world was still stuck in elementary school, China had graduated from college.

Some historians consider the Tang Dynasty to be the greatest period in human civilization. At its height, China was without doubt the most affluent and "modern" place on earth. All roads led to Changan (now Xi'an), which was not just the capital but also the most populated city on earth, and Tang calligraphy, philosophy, and political thought influenced Japan, Korea, and central Asia. Historical records of the Tang upper class show that some lifestyles were opulent. Women had the right to divorce and own property. Paper and movable type were invented during this period. And the Song, too, witnessed a flowering of literature and porcelain making. The Yuan Dynasty, established by the great Mongol warrior Kublai Khan, introduced paper money and dazzled travelers like Marco Polo with its astounding wealth of goods, shops, markets, and enterprise. The dynasty was so efficiently ruled, it was said that during the Yuan period, "A maiden bearing a nugget of gold could wander safely throughout the realm."

The Ming Dynasty extended from 1368 to 1644 and coincided roughly with Europe's age of exploration. In fact, Chinese seagoing junks during this period were four times larger than the ships used by Columbus, and used sophisticated compasses (another Chinese creation). Chinese ships preceded European in exploring the coast of

Africa by a century, and some claim these ships even reached the Americas. But the Chinese came and left without claiming territory, and soon shunned further contact, retreating into a static period of isolation.

By the time the British arrived, China could only yield up its treasures, cede territory, and suffer the widespread introduction of opium. While the West was inventing engines to power its Industrial Revolution, the Qing Dynasty was merely lingering—until its fall in 1911. Students and intellectuals hoped for a new China guided by scientific progress and humanist values. But for China to finally "wake up," as Napoléon had warned, it would take nearly all of the rest of a tumultuous century. Warlords, invasion by Japan, and the civil war that ended in a 1949 Communist victory: all of this hardly did much for the investment climate, either.

Judgments about China's revolutionary leader, Mao Zedong, are guided more by emotions than fact at this point. Nobody, not even China's Communist Party, denies that he made large-scale "mistakes." He rushed industrialization by ordering peasants to somehow make steel by melting down their forks and spoons. And he wasted the country's best and brightest minds by forcing them out of school and into labor camps. The wily Chairman's many erratic crusades and purges, and his ill-conceived one-man management, left millions starving and persecuted—and he nearly bankrupted the country despite decades of factory-building. But some argue that China's Communist regime set the stage for much-delayed development by promoting modern science. There are those who say that while Mao and company established a regime that placed collective will and obedience above personal initiative, the People's Republic, inadvertently or not, freed common people from ancient forms of fatalism and feudal exploitation. Quite accidentally, this new mind-set would give people the confidence to thrive in the kind of market-based economy that has led to the booming of China today.

Before 1949, the Chinese managed steel plants and coal mines. In partnership with their countrymen gone overseas, they established one of the world's most active networks of import and export. And their evident zeal for commerce was not so much stopped during forty years of state socialism, just given a breather.

As China has become strong and whole, the mainland is buttressed by a "Greater China," of which few Americans are even aware. First, there is Taiwan, currently the second-largest contributor to China's inflow of foreign direct investment, second only to Hong Kong. Ever since the Taiwanese government lifted restrictions on investing in the People's Republic in 2001, thousands of Taiwanese-owned businesses have flooded the mainland to take advantage of lower production costs.

Reacquiring Hong Kong in 1997 was hardly symbolic: by 2001, Hong Kong had invested nearly US$175 billion on the mainland. And no price tag can be put on the banking and investment experience found in Hong Kong, which was built up by Shanghainese once fleeing the Communist regime. Even far-off Singapore, a powerful Chinese enclave, has close and productive ties with the mainland.

Then there's China's biggest ally, a nation without borders known in China as "our overseas compatriots." The product of a giant diaspora from a time when China was a poverty-stricken place to flee, there are an estimated sixty-five million ethnic Chinese living around the world. (There are eleven million from Fujian alone.) And they didn't uproot themselves just to introduce the world to wonton soup. In 2000, it was estimated that these immigrants taken collectively have an annual gross domestic product (GDP) of US$45 billion, not that far behind a country like Australia. In Southeast Asia, especially, tiny minorities of Chinese have held large controlling interests in economies, provoking resentments and violent pogroms. Thailand has the largest number of ethnic Chinese, who are estimated to account for 85 percent of the country's wealth. There is similar domination in Malaysia, Indonesia, and the Philippines. These people aren't just open to trading with their ancestral homeland, but are returning Western-educated offspring with capital and experience to help build the nation their families once left.

Beyond all these advances and resources, China has growing intellectual capital. That this is a culture that has always put the highest value and priority on learning is obvious; just look, as I have, at the vast grounds of the birthplace of Confucius in Qufu, stuffed with stone tablets that pay honor to bright scholars as other societies did to cruel warriors. Today, China's best and brightest flood the MIT's and Oxfords of the world. Even within China, universities produce over four hundred thousand engineering graduates per year, compared to two hundred thousand in Japan, eighty thousand in India, and sixty thousand in the United States. As China's white-collar workforce becomes even more educated, and the likes of Intel and Motorola move research facilities to China in order to take advantage of lower costs, the people who invented gunpowder and printing will be seeking new solutions in energy, technology, even outer space.

It could be argued that China is still recovering from the fear and regimentation of the Communist epoch, and is too imitative of the West in its offerings. Certainly, the engine of Chinese innovation is only now just being revved up. But who would bet against the country that first conceived the wheelbarrow, the stirrup and harness, iron casting and the blast furnace, fireworks and cannons, acupuncture, the clock, the kite, the fan, playing cards, the yo-yo, the rudder and the compass, the planetarium, and the first prototypes of propellers?

China's size and the grand sweep of its past give Chinese start-ups another advantage: ambition on an abundant scale. When Silicon Valley executives set a goal of being the best in California, they are still talking about a smaller population than any one Chinese province. For China's managerial classes, it's not at all daunting to plan in terms of big numbers like a hundred thousand employees or a hundred million units.

Many Chinese are making fortunes overnight, the same way immigrants to the United States did when getting in the ground floor of a vast expansion. Out in Chengdu in Sichuan province, there's a fellow named Deng Hong who might as well be called Horatio Alger. As a young man, he went to the United States to make his fortune, but returned to his hometown with fifty dollars to his name. Today, this real estate baron has built the largest convention center in Asia, which is surrounded by a veritable forest transplanted from Tibet and has rooms for fifty thousand people.

In the same city, Fan Jianchuan, who spent eleven years as a poor soldier on China's northern frontier, has plowed much of an immense fortune made in the property market back into creating the Jianchuan

Museum Town, twenty-three separate buildings. This may be the largest private exhibit space in the world and will house his vast collection of twentieth-century historical artifacts. Remember the saying "Only in America"? Now these things can happen only in China. Now it's here that you will find people who dream in full widescreen Technicolor.

The rest of the world has always paid attention to, and been affected by, what happens in China. This is not the first time that China has interacted with the West, but the links are stronger now, the productive capacity far greater. With communications and commerce on a global scale, China's obvious strengths will be magnified—and its gifts could be prodigious.

Jim's Sino Files: Five Modern Chinese Innovators

Focus Media Holding Ltd.
NASDAQ: FMCN
Three-year trend: profits up 230.39 percent, revenues up 630.2 percent

An only-in-China success begun as one thirty-two-year-old's idea to hang video screens inside slow-moving elevators, Focus Media has grown to more than 85,000 display units and 99,700 frames for posters throughout China's malls, airports, etc. Since securing trial deals in fifty Shanghai buildings, Focus Media now bills itself as China's "largest out-of-home multi-platform life-style media company." After raising US$127 million with its 2005 U.S. listing, the company has begun acquiring rivals and is branching into Internet advertising as well.

Baidu.com Inc.
NASDAQ: BIDU, ADR
Three-year trend: profits up 2,412.7 percent, revenues up 613.4 percent

China's Google, founded in 2000, Baidu is the leading search engine for the Chinese market, accounting for 62.1 percent of recent market share—a market with 137 million users, as of May 2007—according to the China Internet Network Information Center (CNNIC). Baidu's plan is to offer search tools suited to Chinese interests and the Chinese language, though it has announced plans to enter Japan and Vietnam. It is starting a music service with EMI and entering into agreements with Chinese universities to try to beat Google in establishing the country's first online library.

China TechFaith Wireless Comm. Technology Ltd.
NASDAQ: CNTF, ADR
Three-year trend: profits up 735 percent, revenues up 831.1 percent

Intel and Qualcomm are strategic investors in this telecom company founded in 2002. An astonishing 90 percent of TechFaith's employees reportedly are engineers. They specialize in handset design, smart phones, and software—in a country with the world's most mobile phones. They also sell in Europe and have entered into partnerships with some of the top foreign names, including Philips and NEC.

Suntech Power Holdings Co., Ltd.
NYSE: STP, ADR
Three-year trend: profits up 476.9 percent, revenues up 602.2 percent

As will be discussed later, China is quickly becoming a world leader in the manufacture and use of solar energy technology. Founded in 2001 by a distinguished scientist researching photovoltaic (PV) cells, Suntech has become one of the world's top ten manufacturers of such cells. The company also produces related "green" technologies. And when it comes to Beijing's "Green" Olympics, Suntech cells will provide energy for the stadiums.

Alibaba Group
Unlisted, planning Hong Kong IPO
Three-year trend: profits and revenues not publicly disclosed

Founded by English teacher Jack Ma as a business-to-business e-commerce platform for small Chinese manufacturers seeking overseas buyers. With several rounds of investment from private equity funds, Alibaba grew into a multiplatform e-commerce firm, including Taobao, an online auction site similar to eBay that's number one in China, and AliPay, a third-party online payment system similar to PayPal. The latter has thrived as a system of guaranteeing arrival of purchases, because many in China still do not have credit cards. Yahoo! paid Alibaba US$1 billion for a 40 percent share in Alibaba, with Alibaba taking over management of Yahoo!'s problematic Chinese subsidiary.

Dialing for Yuan

So how do you choose among companies that are rooted in ancient practices but that were barely a gleam in some young Red Guard's eye thirty years ago?

If today's Chinese executives can call on long-held traditions, they also have young perspectives on the new millennium. Chinese companies, used to working with the basics, can glimpse potential growth in their homeland as well as seize opportunities in Africa or even South America, markets that Western conglomerates might consider "backward." By the same token, domestic companies can sometimes be more adaptive to local tastes. In 1999, the Chinese PC maker Lenovo, which bought out IBM's PC division, created a home computer that became a surprise hit in rural areas. This PC's red color and marketing name, Heavenly Auspicious, were considered lucky, and fathers bought them to give away as bridal dowries.

Motorola, the leader in China for headsets and phone accessories, is losing market share to domestic Chinese firms like Ningbo Bird—whose name may not roll off the tongue but who can respond more quickly to consumer tastes. Back in 1999, the Chinese government chose nine firms to enter the mobile phone field, and Ningbo Bird was the only one that wasn't state-owned. The company chose wisely to become a leading manufacturer of pagers—I recall they used to be so popular in China that every proud office worker carried one strapped to his or her belt. Building on that platform, they sought smaller foreign partners eager to enter the China market, like Sagem and BenQ, then built up their own research departments. Today, Ningbo Bird has been concentrating its sales force on smaller towns that bigger companies sometimes ignore, as well as beefing up their models with popular messaging features.

Still, I think it would be dangerously naïve to presume Chinese companies have some sort of innate leg up. As many a foreign corporation can already attest, you don't need a Confucianist outlook to succeed in China. Three years after the 2002 publication of a book characterizing China as a fantasy that would turn into a nightmare for General Motors and other foreign investors, GM reported that their vehicle sales in China had grown 35 percent from the year before to 665,390 units. GM now makes more money in China than in North America. Western companies have managed to break in quite nicely to many diverse markets throughout the world and are certainly doing the same in China. Some predicted that lactose-intolerant Chinese would never be able to accept all the cheese on pizza—but don't tell that to Pizza Hut!

Nor is there always much relevance in whether a company evolved from one of the converted, inefficient SOE's (state-owned enterprises). Americans especially tend to jump to the conclusion that private management is better management. Even in Europe, however, governments still hold a symbolic "golden share" in many companies deemed critical to national prosperity, and have significant influence over them. And SOE contribution to GDP in China, which had fallen to 10 percent a decade back, has now rebounded to 20 percent. In fact, in 2006, the 159 SOE's under government supervision showed a record high profit of US$92.3 billion.

In China, a country where segments of the People's Liberation Army have diversified into industries ranging from silicon chips to nightclubs, some of the most sophisticated managers are found in state ministries. Although cronyism and promotion through seniority was once the normal way to do business, the government board that oversees SOE's has been actively recruiting outstanding young managers, like the CFO's of both Chalco and Shenhua, two companies cited above.

At the same time, you have to read between the lines of profit statements and examine the overall industry involved before determining if that grand-sounding People's Pop-Tart Factory No. 17 is really some obsolete plant in a noncompetitive field being propped up by state support. Some state-dominated firms *are* moldering hot beds of nepotism, others dynamic and well positioned. Look beyond fancy-sounding names on the door to see whether revenues are stagnant or products are in high demand.

Take a look at the industry as a whole first. As I'll highlight, agriculture, tourism, water resources, and selected service industries could have big upsides and may have good chances to weather dips or bubbles. While China's 2001 accession to the WTO means greater access to China by foreign firms and a lowering of the most egregious protective tariffs, it is mostly in newer fields like banking, retailing, and Internet services that local firms will face the greatest challenge from abroad. But there has been little or no impact in some of the most lucrative areas, like consumer goods, electronics, and telecom.

Already, many Chinese firms have claimed commanding positions while today's intense competition will shake out more industry leaders. But in China, as everywhere else, it's good to answer these questions: Does the company have too much debt? Does it have good profit margins? Does it grow nicely? Does its management have strong incentives to succeed (for example, large stock ownership or options)? Does it have strong competition or is it a dominant player? Is it a leader or a follower? Is it in a growing market—for example, iPods instead of horseshoes, BMW's instead of bicycles?

Shopping for Chinese brands is a bit like a trip to the supermarket, whether to Wal-Mart or to Chinese leader Lianhua. Read the labels, check the specials, and, above all, get familiar with what's on the shelves.

4

Energy: Not So Black

If China were one big firm, you'd have to say the fundamentals are looking pretty good. This Communist country has plenty of capital to use for expansion or investment. After years of pulling off an incredibly favorable balance of trade, they've passed Japan and now have the largest currency reserves of any nation. With 40 percent of their output going to exports, they aren't crippled by massive foreign debt. Unlike the United States, where most of the society lives on credit, leaving only 2 percent for the future, the Chinese are funding their own reconstruction—helping strengthen financial institutions and their capital base—through their high savings rates of over 35 percent.

Built with foreign partners to the highest possible standards, China's fixed assets—roads, bridges, and ports—have doubled in capacity every two and a half years for the past two decades. In one recent year, China produced 50 percent of the world's cameras, 30 percent of the world's air conditioners and televisions, and even higher proportions of textiles and toys, with one company making 40 percent of microwaves sold in Europe.

Still, all that productive capacity needs energy when the switch is flipped. As the world's factory transforms into a world superpower, the most critical area to examine—and consider investing in—has to be power itself. As we plug into China's amazing growth trajectory, we must also confront, as China's leaders are already doing, limits in supply and growing environmental concerns. Indeed, the story of the Chinese century may be how a giant destined for greatness had to rethink its energy sources, strategies, and outdated notions of industrial might—and helped save the planet while providing plenty of investment opportunities.

Powering Up

Like a teenager feeding a growth spurt, China has been voraciously consuming energy. The country is used to getting its fill from traditional raw fuels such as coal and crude oil. But recently China has begun to heed its waistline, which is bulging from excess pollution and inefficient delivery. Rocketing world commodity prices are also forcing a country used to cheap and dirty fixes to get more power from hydro, nuclear, wind, and solar sources.

Thus it's not just the oil futures market that will be worth watching in the years ahead, but everything from international companies that provide expertise in building nuclear power, to domestic coal companies, to young start-ups in solar power and wind turbines.

A British investor financed Shanghai's first power plant in 1882, but the Chinese did not even begin a nationwide electricity system until the 1949 founding of the Communist state. Until 1978, the Chinese government provided electricity through state central planning. (Similarly, the United States used government regulation in the 1930s to promote low-cost electricity for rural areas, and even today electricity generation is still a heavily regulated industry.) In 1979 about 40 percent of rural Chinese households still lacked access to electricity; by 2005, estimates had 98 percent of villages electrified—the year that China became the world's second-biggest consumer of electricity.

In the mid-1980s, as the economy began to outgrow its sluggish socialist shell, electricity shortages were so serious that factories often shut production lines four days out of every week. This had the desirable effect of spurring government efforts to decentralize the electricity industry. Even though the government claimed to be a centrally planned economy, by the end of the 1990s, the central government controlled less than 50 percent of China's generating capacity.

The government also began to allow limited freedom in price setting, which had been strictly controlled. But energy's watershed came in 2002, when the Chinese government dismantled the State Power Corporation and reallocated its assets into five provincial companies. These became known collectively as "the Big Five": China Datang Corp., China Power Investment Corp., China Huaneng Group, China Guodian Corp., and China Huadian Corp. (Some branches of these companies, with slightly different names, are in the Sino Files below.)

For the first time, power plants and transmission and distribution utilities became flexible, independent, and competing entities. Furthermore, over fifty partially state-owned or independent plants competed with them head-to-head. This led to increased profits as demand grew with lower prices and greater availability. The reforms also had the unwitting effect of allowing individuals to buy shares in companies benefiting from immense flows of government capital and huge blocks of users.

Meanwhile, the government gradually closed inefficient state-owned factories that had been consuming electricity voraciously. As demand diminished, the government imposed a moratorium on new power plant construction. That moratorium was repealed in January 2002, when the government realized this shortsighted policy did not anticipate the energy needs caused by rapid growth. In 2003, total generating capacity increased by 8 percent while electricity demand increased more than 15 percent. Attempting to prevent blackouts and sudden price hikes, the government rationed electricity while it scrambled to increase capacity by approving dozens of new electric power projects. Still, twenty out of thirty-one provinces experienced chronic electrical shortages in 2004. Twenty-five provinces joined a voluntary arrangement to rotate power supplies in 2005, but few needed that by the year after. By now, Chinese authorities are more worried about a surplus (which some find ludicrous, considering it is all based on projections).

In order to keep pace with the skyrocketing cost of coal, electricity prices were largely deregulated in 2005. And where distant rural residents once had to pay far higher bills than those in the city, costs have more or less evened out since 2004—which has spawned even greater demand across the countryside. Add a lot of new industry, housing, and city lights to this and you've got a problem. The International Energy Agency estimates that to meet its rapidly growing electrical demand, China needs to invest nearly US$2 trillion in electricity infrastructure between 2001 and 2030. This amount represents about one fifth of total world investment in electricity.

Still the mix of fuel sources for electricity generation is undergoing rapid change and therefore must be tracked carefully. While China doesn't have significant reserves of oil or natural gas, nature has provided the country with an abundance of coal. When I first arrived, every Chinese city had yellowish air, and the soot in my lungs gave me a cough. Most homes were still heated with coal I could see being hauled about by bicycle. China consumed 1.53 billion short tons of coal in 2003, 28 percent of the world total. China's total recoverable coal reserves are estimated to be about 126.2 billion short tons, roughly sixty years' supply. Even as China scrambles to add nuclear and hydroelectric power capacity, coal accounts for 70 percent of electricity generation, and rising demand is expected to offset the use of other energy sources so that coal will continue to account for over 60 percent. In the United States, we generate over 50 percent of our electricity from coal.

China produced 2.834 trillion kilowatt-hours (kWh) of electricity in 2006, a yearly increase of 13.5 percent, among which 2.357 trillion kWh came from coal power and only 416.6 kWh came from hydropower. China became a net importer of coal for the first time ever in the first quarter of 2007. And with China leading the way, coal continues to rise in price. In 2006, the S&P Coal and Consumable Fuels index witnessed higher growth than the S&P 500.

Yet, according to the eleventh Five-Year Plan that was approved in 2006 and covers 2007 to 2012, China aims to reduce its coal use by 560 million tons before 2010. The government has ordered big and medium coal-power plants to install desulfurization equipment and has started closing smaller plants to limit pollution. In other words, while the energy pie is growing, coal's slice might narrow in favor of cleaner fuels. So investing in coal producers may make sense for now, though tax policies and conservation issues remain long-term factors. As environmental concerns grow, clean coal-power technologies should be an area to watch, too.

There was only US$200 million in foreign investment in Chinese mines through 2004, and a recent auctioning of three mines in Shaanxi province was canceled when foreign companies dominated bids. But China is becoming more open to foreign investment in the coal sector—in order to speed the modernization and environmental improvement of existing mines.

Despite China's lack of adequate oil and gas reserves, the country's huge coal reserves will continue to ensure growth. Many developed countries are likely to suffer from energy shortages and high prices due to their dependence on oil rather than coal—another reason to consider China, and its position of strength, on a long-term strategic basis.

Jim's Sino Files: Making Juice Flow

Huadian Power International
SHA: 600027, A-shares; HKG: 1071, H-shares; OTC: HPIFF
Three-year trend: profits up 26.8 percent, revenues up 48.7 percent

Most of the Big Five have been allowed several listings in order to raise funds. Huadian is northern Shandong province's largest electricity provider, but also operates in four other provinces, in coordination with nearby coal sources.

Datang International Power Generation
SHA: 601991, A-shares; HKG: 0991, H-shares; OTC: DIPGY
Three-year trend: profits up 30.6 percent, revenues up 82.8 percent

Listed as far back as 1997, Datang manages twenty regional power generation companies and has made investments in hydropower, nuclear power, and wind power. Share prices have continued to rise despite the closing of five plants due to environmental cleanup.

China Power International Development, Ltd.
HKG: 2380, H-shares; OTC: CPWIF
Three-year trend: profits up 10.5 percent, revenues up 55.2 percent

This big player manages nine power plants in eastern China and has been acquiring shares of competitors. Of note is China Power's unusual CEO: young, ambitious, and female. She rose from the ranks of engineers after graduating from Tsinghua University (often described as China's MIT).

GD Power Development Company
SHA: 600795, A-shares
Three-year trend: profits up 19.6 percent, revenues up 70.7 percent

More than fifty smaller electricity generators, some state-owned and some independent, compete with the Big Five. Here's one that has been managing to grow.

Kailuan Clean Coal Co., Ltd.
SHA: 600997, A-shares
Three-year trend: profits up 73.1 percent, revenues up 103.6 percent

With the aforementioned Shenhua (in previous chapter), Kailuan is a comer among the top ten Chinese coal mine operators. In last figures, 93 percent of sales were in the domestic market.

Inner Mongolia Yitai Coal
SHA: 900948, B-shares
Three-year trend: profits up 102.6 percent, revenues up 41.6 percent

For foreign investors, this company may hold romance—as well as few regional competitors. Yitai works in the remote steppes of China's Inner Mongolian Autonomous Region.

Yanzhou Coal Mining Co.
SHA: 600188, A-shares; HKG: 1171, H-shares; NYSE: YZC, ADR; OTC: YZCHF
Three-year trend: profits down 35.4 percent, revenues up 8.3 percent

Runs six large mines and sends some exports to Japan and Korea. Recent losses have been blamed on lower coal prices and an Australian mining division.

Guangxi Liugong Machinery Co., Ltd.
SHE: 000528, A-shares
Three-year trend: profits up 46.3 percent, revenues up 47.7 percent

Mine equipment manufacturers are also riding the coal wave as excavators, hydraulic support systems, and armored face conveyors are put to even greater use. Approximately 90 percent of China's coal is extracted using domestically produced machinery. Guangxi Liugong also generates international sales.

Shantui Construction Machinery Co., Ltd.
SHE: 000680, A-shares
Three-year trend: profits up 160.8 percent, revenues up 80.8 percent

With six major subsidiaries, Shantui offers mining exposure.

Joy Global Inc.
NASDAQ: JOYG
Three-year trend: profits up 652.7 percent, revenues up 67.7 percent

Two thirds of international coal mining machinery exports are sold to China. This is one of the beneficiaries, based in Milwaukee.

Ingersoll-Rand Co., Ltd.
NYSE: IR
Three-year trend: profits down 15.3 percent, revenues up 21.5 percent

The major international manufacturer has a big presence in China. It offers a wide range of industrial technologies, from energy to security systems, but also provides "bobcat" vehicles and construction equipment.

Bucyrus International, Inc.
NASDAQ: BUCY
Three-year trend: profits up 1,056.2 percent, revenues up 62.5 percent

Also based in Wisconsin, Bucyrus makes machinery primarily for surface mining.

Gushing with Pride

Of course, there's another black substance that is even more critical to China's future. From the Middle East to Latin America to the tip of Africa to the former Soviet republics, Chinese companies have been staking out economic interests and diplomatic relationships in not so subtle pursuit of oil. The Russian and Chinese governments have been holding regular discussions on the feasibility of pipelines to make increased exports from Siberia. An even more controversial pipeline to China from central Asia has been in the planning stages for a decade now. And Venezuelan president Hugo Chávez is moving toward putting his country's huge reserves at China's disposal as a way of thumbing his nose at the United States. Just as the creation of OPEC (the Organization of the Petroleum Exporting Countries) has impacted every country on earth for decades, China's oil needs will rearrange world politics.

Since 1992, China's consumption of oil has more than doubled, to more than 5.4 million barrels per day according to International Energy Agency (IEA) data. China now consumes only 8 percent of the world's oil, but it also accounted for about 40 percent of the growth in consumption during the first four years of the new millennium. If such demand keeps growing at an average rate of 6 to 7 percent a year (as it has since 1990), China's demand will be matching the current consumption levels of the United States—of twenty-one million barrels a day—in less than twenty years.

And China is really still a toddler when it comes to gas guzzling. That could either be seen as promising or frightening (depending on whether or not you work for oil companies or invest in them). As of 2005, China still consumed barely one third the amount the United States consumed, making it a very distant third, after the United States and the EU, in terms of total consumption. China ranked only 136th in the world in terms of barrels per day per person. Japan ranked thirty-second, and South Korea ranked thirty-first, consuming ten times more barrels per day per person than China.

With proven oil reserves of around 18.3 billion barrels amounting to less than five years' supply—unless recent big finds pan out—China is now scrambling to form alliances with oil-rich countries (like Saudi Arabia and Russia), companies, and individuals. In 2004, China also began a series of overseas acquisition attempts specifically aimed at foreign oil companies as well as other commodity companies. State-owned firms have spent about US$5 billion acquiring oil and gas fields overseas in the past ten years alone, and with its over one trillion U.S. dollars in foreign reserves, China is willing and able to spend a lot more in the years ahead.

In the wake of restructuring and privatization in 1998, three major oil and gas companies were established in China. These are far more dominant than the power companies and they account for nearly all the country's refining as well as natural gas capacity. These former state entities are also more interrelated: top executives from one have actually switched places with another. The China National Petroleum Corporation (CNPC), for example, is the largest producer of crude oil and natural gas in Asia. CNPC is also the largest transporter and seller of natural gas in China and the second-largest manufacturer of chemicals in China. CNPC was created to service the north and west of the country, although this geographic area is now not a restriction but only a guideline. These vertically integrated companies stand to benefit from increasing demand, pricing power, and their connections.

China Petrochemical Corporation, known as Sinopec, is an even more aggressive firm—exploring petrochemical, fiber, and chemical fertilizer production. Finally, China National Offshore Oil Corporation (CNOOC) accounts for more than 10 percent of China's domestic crude oil production. Currently the only company permitted to conduct exploration and production activities with foreign oil and gas companies off China's coastlines, CNOOC has built a reputation as being acquisitive, carving out interests in Indonesia, Australia, central Asia, and Africa. The company made headlines in 2005 by bidding US$18.5 billion for California-based Unocal. After encountering intense opposition in the U.S. Congress, CNOOC rescinded their offer with some shock. If they couldn't look to the United States for a model of free markets, where could they?

All three of these companies wield critical influence on China's economy. All three companies carried out highly successful initial public offerings between 2000 and 2002, bringing in billions of dollars in foreign capital. Yet for all the attention and controversy stemming from Chinese companies' investments in overseas oil, these companies' total contribution to China's oil imports was still well under three hundred thousand barrels per day as of mid-2005. These are a drop in the bucket compared to China's daily imports of 3.5 million barrels per day. Despite China's efforts to diversify its supply sources, roughly half of the country's imported oil comes from the Middle East, with Saudi Arabia alone accounting for 17 percent.

In 2005, Chinese officials commenced construction of a one-hundred-million-barrel national strategic petroleum reserve. This will be China's lifeline in the event of a global energy crisis, although it is far from an adequate emergency supply (less than a month's worth of consumption). But China's oil refineries are among its best-managed enterprises. The companies have been steadily eliminating many unprofitable ancillary activities. Layoffs have also been undertaken, since, as with many other Chinese state enterprises, the companies were overstaffed.

Some investors may feel it is enough to hold shares in international oil companies to benefit from China's growth, but it is important to realize that these companies will be dependent on Chinese firms to establish footholds in China. Even when Shell sets up an offshore drill or ExxonMobil invests in a trans-Asian pipeline, China's government will favor its own oil companies (as do other governments all over the world). All three of the global companies—BP, ExxonMobil, and Shell—intend to enter the Chinese retail market in partnership with CNPC, Sinopec, or both. Chinese firms have set up incredibly favorable conditions in their joint ventures with foreign firms. CNOOC has the right to 51 percent of any foreign partner's finds along China's coastline.

Analysts are also concerned that the Chinese government will continue to keep petroleum prices artificially low. Due to price controls, China's gasoline prices rank with those of the United States as among the world's lowest for oil-importing countries. They are about one third of those in Europe, where taxes inflate prices. The Chinese government, however, has shown a willingness to let gas prices climb at the pump, both to regulate oil use and to help Chinese oil companies stay profitable. In the first half of 2005, the government grew alarmed as the gap expanded between the prices of domestic oil and world oil—and China's oil companies boosted exports of some petroleum products, particularly diesel, to cash in on better prices for these products on the world market. Even the Communist government recognized the handsome profits to be realized. So the government responded by allowing gas pump prices and petroleum product prices to increase throughout 2005 and 2006, and eventually they will eliminate subsidized prices.

One thing is certain: China's days as a net exporter of crude oil are over and the country's voracious demand for imports will make China a decisive player in international oil markets. When China is thirsty, the price will go up, and when China hiccups, so will the oil markets.

Jim's Sino Files: Slick Oil Stocks

PetroChina Co., Ltd.
HKG: 0857, H-shares; NYSE: PTR, ADR; OTC: PCCYF
Three-year trend: profits up 38.8 percent, revenues up 73.4 percent

China's big oil companies generate appropriately big stocks. With annual returns of 26-plus percent, PetroChina is frequently included in mutual funds. Largest foreign shareholders include BP Amoco and Berkshire Hathaway.

In the 2006 "Forbes 2000" rankings of leading companies, PetroChina ranked first among Chinese companies and fifty-fifth worldwide. Some think it could go higher: in March 2007, the company reported discovery of the largest offshore field in Asia in the past thirty-three years.

China National Petroleum Corp.

HKG: 0135, H-shares

Three-year trend: profits up 155.8 percent, revenues up 53.7 percent

CNPC has acquired oil concessions in Azerbaijan, Canada, Kazakhstan, Venezuela, Sudan, Indonesia, Iraq, and Iran. Despite negative press (some allege that CNPC is indirectly funding Sudan's genocide), the Greater Nile Petroleum Operating Company (GNPOC), the Sudanese oil project in which CNPC owns a stake, began exports to China in 1999. (But there is no real evidence it is financing genocide. As Warren Buffett argued at an annual meeting where investment in CNPC was approved, the Chinese firm is not the parent company in this case, but has a subsidiary interest.) CNPC has also set up subsidiaries for drilling services and geological survey work, and plans to spin them off into international IPO's.

China Petroleum & Chemical Corporation (Sinopec)

SHA: 600028, A-shares; HKG: 0386, H-shares; NYSE: SNP, ADR

Three-year trend: profits up 32.6 percent, revenues up 74.9 percent

China's largest producer and marketer of oil products such as gasoline, diesel fuel, jet fuel, chemical fibers, and chemical fertilizers — which account for one third of its revenue. Though created to service China's southern region, Sinopec is now national in scope and has begun purchasing oil assets overseas. Its most notable success is the development of Iran's Yadavaran oil field, which could eventually produce three hundred thousand barrels per day. On the other side of the globe, Sinopec also acquired a 40 percent stake in Canada's Northern Lights tar sands project.

China National Offshore Oil Corp.
HKG: 0883, H-shares; NYSE: CEO, ADR
Three-year trend: profits up 91.6 percent, revenues up 61.1 percent

Its bid for Unocal, the sixth-largest U.S. oil company with its large Southeast Asian reserves, was blocked by the U.S. Congress in 2005 but helped put the company on the global stage. CNOOC began in the mid-eighties, when China first opened its national reserves for exploration—with the company getting half of all finds.

China Oilfield Services Limited (COSL)
HKG: 2883, H-shares; OTC: CHOLF, CHOLY
Three-year trend: profits up 60.8 percent, revenues up 66.4 percent

A separate oil field division of CNOOC worth noting, it is planning a Shanghai listing as well.

Generating Alternatives

Say the word "China" and most people think of smokestacks belching out greenhouse gases, dirty rivers and skies, a black mark on the world. But in fact, China started thinking about cleaning up its act before they began to trumpet their "green" Olympics.

In February 2005, the Chinese government passed a law requiring that renewable energy resources generate 10 percent of China's energy by 2020. Furthermore, in January 2006, China's renewable energy law went into effect, requiring large provincial utilities to sign agreements with at least one wind-power-generating company to purchase all of its generated energy. And the government plans to spend US$200 billion alone on renewable energy over the next fifteen years. These are more than token efforts. As Reuters pointed out in July

2006: "That kind of money would buy you an oil firm the size of Chevron and leave change to fund the current renewable programs of all Europe's top oil firms for 25 years."

As pressure grows to decrease global warming, and coal reserves have to be shipped farther, nuclear power will come to be seen as a cleaner and ultimately cheaper choice. In 2006, China's installed power generation capacity reached 508.41 million kilowatts, up 14.9 percent from 2005, yet nuclear power accounted for only 4 percent of total power generation. Today, about 16 percent of the world's electricity supply comes from nuclear power, but nearly 80 percent of the 441 commercial nuclear reactors worldwide are more than fifteen years old. To maintain nuclear power's position in the overall energy mix, new reactors will have to replace decommissioned ones. China has ten reactors in operation, and at least four more under construction, and plans on building twenty-five more nuclear power plants by 2020.

Hydroelectric projects are also a big part of China's plan to reduce dependence on coal and oil. Throughout the world, the electricity produced from hydropower stations is equivalent to 4.4 million barrels of oil each day. Current and projected high oil prices have made hydropower an even more crucial energy source particularly for oil-importing developing countries like China. The Chinese government is seeking a 40 percent increase in hydropower generation, to add to an overall mix of 16 percent from renewable resources by 2020.

Surprisingly, given its eternal obsession with controlling flooding rivers and irrigation fields, hydropower development in China still has a way to go. But if anyone still doubts China is serious about both its energy needs and its infrastructure, the controversial Three Gorges Dam may change their mind. Long proposed, and actively planned since 1954, the dam is the single most costly construction project in history.

The idea of building a dam across the Yangtze River to control flooding and to harness it for hydropower has been the dream of several generations of Chinese since the time of Dr. Sun Yat-sen, forerunner of China's democratic revolution. Since 1954, Chinese and foreign scientists and engineers have devoted themselves to the planning, design, and consulting work of the project. Construction began in 1994. The reservoir began filling on June 1, 2003, and structural work was finished on May 20, 2006, nine months ahead of schedule. However, several generators still have to be installed, and the dam is not expected to become fully operational until about 2009.

This has not been achieved without cost to people and the environment. The project displaced 1.9 million people, destroyed natural and archaeological wonders, and may yet cause further problems. What's certain is that the Three Gorges Dam will be the largest hydropower station and dam in the world, with a 1.2-mile stretch of concrete and a 370-mile-long reservoir that is 525 feet deep. It will produce the energy of fifteen nuclear power plants and is the largest hydroelectric river dam in the world, more than five times the size of Hoover Dam.

With less fanfare, China has executed another large hydropower project involving a series of dams on the upper portion of the Yellow River. Shaanxi (a central province with thirty-seven million people), Qinghai (a western province with five million people), and Gansu (a western province with twenty-six million people) have jointly created the Yellow River Hydroelectric Development Corporation, with plans for the eventual construction of twenty-five generating stations. At this point, the Yellow River Hydroelectric Development Corporation is not publicly traded, and there has been no indication that it intends to raise capital on public markets.

During one of my recent trips to China, I noticed odd fixtures on the rooftops of many of the stately old homes in Shanghai's former French Concession (as the areas controlled by foreign powers were once called). At first, I thought these contraptions were some kind of extraneous status symbols, before realizing they had to be sheets of solar paneling. As I discovered, solar-powered household appliances have become all the rage in China. Today, China uses more household solar energy per capita than any other country in the world.

In rural and urban China alike, solar-generated hot water is more economical than any other sources. This has spawned a huge industry practically overnight—employing eight hundred thousand people as of 2005 and generating US$1.9 billion. Still, less than 8 percent of total households utilize solar heaters. So there's plenty of room for growth in companies offering such new technologies, especially in the midst of a real estate construction boom.

In Shanghai, the city government has undertaken thirty projects that integrate urban infrastructure with solar energy. The city now pledges to install one hundred thousand solar panels, while neighboring Jiangsu province will add fifty thousand. Beijing has announced plans to build a "solar street" where buildings, lights, and other features will run entirely on solar energy. And Olympic planners intend to use solar power generators at the Olympic venues in 2008.

China has natural advantages in this area, too. Two thirds of China's land area receives more than two thousand hours of sunlight annually, more than many other regions of similar latitude, including Europe and Japan. In line with the country's development strategy for the more rural western regions, the country has invested US$241 million in solar energy power plants in western rural towns.

As I mentioned, the Chinese government has also done much to encourage the wind-power sector. It halved the tax rate that wind farms face and similarly reduced the import custom tariff on wind turbine generators from 12 percent to 6 percent. As a result, more than thirty power companies, including the Big Five electricity utilities, are building wind farms in China and have cumulatively invested more than US$1.24 billion.

In recent years, China's wind-power capacity has been increasing at rapid rates. With large deserts in the west, and strong air currents coming down from Siberia, China has large potential in this area as well. As of late 2005, China had installed 1,864 turbines, with a cumulative capacity of 1,270 megawatts, but that capacity doubled by 2006, with sixty-one wind farms increasing to ninety-two. At the moment, China is harnessing only one thousandth of its potential wind energy, and will need to invest US$12.5 billion just to meet goals. Demand will continue to skyrocket as the government works to meet its target of thirty gigawatts of cumulative installed turbine capacity by 2020. If China's wind-power initiatives unfold as planned, wind power will replace hydropower as the third-largest source of electricity by that time—topping even nuclear power.

Better still for Chinese firms, the government has mandated that equipment be three quarters Chinese-produced, where it is only one quarter now. One way to invest in wind power is to consider companies that produce the turbines for wind farms. Since the 1990s, major European turbine manufacturers have beaten their domestic Chinese competitors in price because of government subsidies within the European Union. And Chinese turbine makers still lag behind their European counterparts in both technology and scale. If these companies catch up, they might become some of the most profitable businesses in the world's wind-power sector. Cheaper Chinese alternatives would significantly increase profit margins of Chinese wind-power producers. When domestic wind turbine companies and wind-power companies start to list on exchanges, investors should catch the breeze.

China's commitment to renewable energy in the coming decades will alter energy consumption and stimulate energy technologies around the world. The amounts of money going into the sector are staggering. Should it change your portfolio?

Jim's Sino Files: Blowin' in China's Wind

AREVA
EPA: 004524; OTC (Over-the-Counter): ARVCF
Three-year trend: profits up 43.9 percent, revenues down 7.2 percent

The state-owned China National Nuclear Corporation (CNNC), which controls nearly all development in nuclear energy, is not publicly traded—though there are periodic reports that they may restructure some civilian branches in preparation for listing. So investors seeking some secondary benefit from nuclear expansion need to look at foreign companies that supply China with nuclear technology and equipment. AREVA, a French firm that built the first Chinese nuclear plant near Hong Kong, has significant plans for expansion in China. Also keep an eye on Westinghouse, now a subsidiary of Toshiba (TYO [Tokyo]: 6502; OTC: TOSBF), which is among those bidding on two new plants costing up to US$7 billion.

SUFA Technology Industry Co., Ltd.
SHE: 000777, A-shares

Three-year trend: profits up 94.3 percent, revenues up 20.1 percent

SUFA is the main valve manufacturer for China's nuclear plants and the only listed company affiliated to the CNNC.

USEC Inc.
NYSE: USU

Three-year trend: profits up 365.6 percent, revenues up 30.4 percent

This American mining and enrichment firm is one of many that could benefit from China's increasing need for uranium. Canada also produces a third of the world's needs, and Cameco (NYSE: CCJ) is one important producer. There are also mining-related ETF's like SPDR S&P Mining and Metals (AMEX: SME), some with uranium stocks. The Uranium Participation Corporation (trades as a commodity ETF: TSX.U) on the Toronto Exchange.

BHP Billiton Ltd.
ASX (Australian Securities Exchange): BHP; NYSE: BHP, BBL (ADR); OTC: BHPBF

Three-year trend: profits up 224.2 percent, revenues up 40.5 percent

It's Australia, however, that produces 40 percent of the world's uranium, and BHP is a main Australian producer. The country has just agreed to start shipping large amounts to China after 2010, so long as the uranium is used for peaceful purposes.

Dongfang Electrical Machinery Co., Ltd.
SHA: 600875, A-shares; HKG: 1072, H-shares

Three-year trend: profits up 213.6 percent, revenues up 129 percent

Dongfang Electrical specializes in large generators and has seen consistently high share returns.

Sichuan Minjiang Hydropower Company
SHA: 600131, A-shares
Three-year trend: profits up 477.9 percent, revenues up 86.5 percent

Just under the radar of the Big Five electric companies, this provincial company has done well by investing heavily in hydropower.

China Yangtze Power Co.
SHA: 600900, A-shares
Three-year trend: profits up 19.1 percent, revenues up 21.2 percent

For investors with a sense of history, this is the way to participate in the earthshaking (literally) Three Gorges Dam, which is starting to churn along.

ABB
NYSE: ABB, ADR (Also on Swiss and Swedish exchanges)
Three-year trend: profits up 219.1 percent, revenues up 21.2 percent

This Swiss construction group won a US$390 million contract for work on the Three Gorges project, and achieved sales of US$2.8 billion in China in 2006, with a goal of doubling this figure through hydroelectric bids.

Jiangsu Sunshine Company
SHA: 600220, A-shares
Three-year trend: profits up 70.2 percent, revenues up 17 percent

With a solar gold rush under way, the solar energy market is one of the most competitive in China. Buoyed by government support and bolstered by worldwide demand, the entire industry's projected growth is between 20 and 30 percent. Picking among the dozens of firms popping up every few months requires plenty of homework. I've already highlighted Suntech as one of China's major brands, but Jiangsu Sunshine is a textile company that has put a large investment into becoming one of the world's largest solar cell manufacturers, after striking an alliance with a professor who has patented cells that he claims double the output of current technologies.

Trina Solar
NASDAQ: TSL
Three-year trend: profits US$13.17 million up from US$370,000 loss, revenues up 27,826.8 percent

Shares soon fell after Trina's 2006 IPO. The company supplies solar modules to many companies, particularly in Germany, and designs overall solar systems. Another new entry, LDK Solar Hi-Tech, should already have an IPO on the NASDAQ when this publishes. This solar wafer maker in Jiangxi province has opened numerous R&D centers including ones in Sydney, Australia, and Sunnyvale, California.

Huangshi Dongbei Electrical Appliance Company
SHA: 900956, B-shares
Three-year trend: profits up 600.6 percent, revenues up 90.4 percent

A mainstream appliance manufacturer, known mainly for refrigerator compressors, they have started a line of solar-powered appliances. Three thousand Chinese companies manufacture solar-powered water heaters. Most are small, unlisted companies like Five Star, Himin Solar Energy Group, Singhua Yang Guang—watch for these.

Guodian Changyuan Electric Power Company
SHE: 000966, A-shares
Three-year trend: profits down 10.4 percent, revenues up 2,462.4 percent

Guodian Changyuan's subsidiary, Longyuan Power Company, is responsible for 46 percent of China's wind-power output. China Datang, described under "Powering Up," has also invested in wind farms.

REpower Systems AG
FRA (Frankfurt Stock Exchange): RPW
Three-year trend: profits US$9.7 million up from US$13.2 million loss,
revenues up 53.1 percent

Chinese manufacturers are still struggling to break into their own nation's lucrative wind turbine industry. German REpower Systems has signed a licensing agreement with Dongfang Steam Turbine Works, not yet publicly traded, a state-owned company in southwest China that accounted for 30 percent of the domestic turbine market. GoldWind Science and Technology, China's largest domestic turbine manufacturer, not yet listed, has also been purchasing designs from REpower. GoldWind is based in Urumqi, in China's far west—where there is plenty of wind and not much else.

5

Transport: Paving the Way

Of all the strange sights encountered when I first hit China's roads, the strangest may have been what I didn't see at all. Beijing, Shanghai, and Guangzhou, megacities of ten and more million, still had no traffic jams because there was no traffic—in fact, almost no private cars. The "ring roads" that form a giant Chinese box around China's capital, built by Mao to replace the ancient city wall he tore down, seemed more for show than actual use. A few Liberation-brand trucks puttered along, and with the first Western tourists, taxis appeared to join the slow-motion procession down eerily empty lanes. At night, rebellious rockers took to sprinting down the dividers for fun. But maybe they, and Chinese planners, knew what was coming. Today, rush hour in the Forbidden City is no more fun than it is in the Big Apple.

Just a few years back, China was a country that moved on two wheels. But patient commuters pedaling in great waves on their "Flying Pigeons" bicycles have now been consigned to side lanes. Of course, China still manufactured eighty million bicycles in 2006, accounting for 80 percent of global production (and the Chinese dominate motorbike production as well). But for a lot of Chinese these days, the bike is a second choice to keep in the trunk. Government officials promoting car-free days, to fight pollution before Beijing's Olympics, make headlines for doing something that was ordinary just a few years back—riding their bicycles to work.

China's auto industry is growing faster than the economy as a whole, and that takes some doing. In 2006, China streaked ahead of Japan to become the world's number two market for automobiles. And China, with an annual output of fifteen million units, is expected to surpass the United States as the world's top car producer by 2020. Already, China has more car brands on the market than America. But there are still plenty of potential two-car garages in Chinese cities that do not even hold one. And out in the countryside, there are myriad millions of miles of road yet to be conquered by the best contraptions designed in Detroit and Tokyo.

Looking at China today, I see the United States a hundred years back, before Henry Ford even got started with his Model T, or Japan just recovering from the Second World War. There are a whole lot of consumers and truckers who have yet to be put behind the wheel. And that leaves a lot of room on the road to future growth: for every one thousand people, the United States has seven hundred cars. At last count, and despite the increased congestion, China had only twenty-four cars per thousand people.

So long, trusty bicycle. Hello, sexy sedans and Chinese convertibles. Even if the scramble to establish local car brands leads at first to overcapacity and a glut of mini-jalopies, such affordable wheels will only mean higher revenues for roads, road-builders, auto parts and repair, suppliers, and allied tourism. Either way, there are big gains to be had from China climbing into the driver's seat of the world auto industry.

Road Warriors

The first time I drove across China in 1988, I was lucky to survive the trip. China did not have a single expressway then. I was spinning my wheels on rough desert sands and wondering how I would ever make it. I forded muddy streams and weaved around gaping cracks in the road that truckers had to wait days to traverse. Now the cross-country route is paved entirely. The Chinese have learned how to create highways from the Germans, the Japanese, and the Americans. In short order, they have quickly built a procession of toll roads—up to 122 at the end of 2006—that are new, clean, and state-of-the-art. Yes, comrades, toll roads! "If you want to pass here, show me the money!" another Chinese saying goes. Only now, it's not bandits but road builders who collect.

There's no law of nature that says the best highways can only be built by people in cowboy hats and Chevy trucks. Long before the West did, China created wonders in civil engineering: colossal waterway systems like the 1,114-mile-long Grand Canal, by far the world's biggest, begun in 486 B.C. with twenty-four locks and some sixty bridges. And of course the 3,946-mile Great Wall—which, sorry folks, cannot actually be seen from space but was viewed by Richard Nixon, who duly observed, "It really is a great wall."

Under socialism, the slogan of China's forced industrialization was "China Reconstructs." Today, the operative phrase is more like "Highways to Heaven." With 28,210 miles of highways at the end of 2006, China boasted the world's second-longest set of freeways, roughly equal to those of Canada, Germany, and France combined. In the last four years, about 3,000 miles of expressways were added each year on average. And there are plans afoot to construct and pave up to triple the current number.

They may end up looking even more like America's roads, thanks to an announcement that McDonald's will build thirty thousand drive-throughs as adjuncts to the Sinopec gas stations that line major highways. (As some foreign companies seek to exploit the gasoline market, a major source of profits in the West, retailing and franchising at stations with good traffic and locations are just being considered in China.)

Rural highway building was also considered a key aspect of the national poverty reduction program that lifted eighty million people out of subsistence from 1994 to 2000. Highways quickly blur the distinctions between urban and rural China. For example, the Longgang development area near Wenzhou, with a population nearing one million, is a town settled by peasants leaving unproductive land and "coming down from the mountain." One hundred forty thousand inhabitants now get urban services there.

To support this expansion, the Chinese government is steadily revising laws and regulations to make foreign investment more attractive and the regulations more transparent for investors, particularly institutional investors with the financial clout to fund massive projects. Until recently, foreign firms, mostly from Hong Kong and Taiwan, were allowed to form joint ventures with Chinese companies to develop highway systems, communication systems, postal service systems, and a variety of other infrastructure projects. Many local governments offer tax waivers and paybacks for foreign investors in infrastructure projects such as toll roads and airports.

Heavily funded by the Communist Party, China's road to highway construction has been made bumpy by corrupt politicians taking advantage of rural constituents. In one highly publicized case, an official in charge of the expressways in Sichuan province was put to death for accepting bribes. By the same token, management in charge of Zhejiang province's road building suddenly announced acquisition of a brokerage house in 2006, a move so far from their core competency that it led to a stock sell-off.

In this modernizing country, the need for new infrastructure can only grow. Beijing will invest some US$33.7 billion for the 2008 Olympics alone, 64.3 percent of it devoted to construction. It is possible that there will be a letdown in the building industry after the Olympic boom is completed, perhaps even excess capacity as has happened in other countries after their Olympics. But there is hardly a Chinese city worth its socks that hasn't got a new civic center, road, or port or embankment or major housing project in blueprints. China is so vast, and has plans so ambitious, that it is hard to imagine its infrastructure sector will run out of new things to build.

And this is one place where you don't have to put your hard-earned cash in the pockets of used-car salesmen. In China, you can actually invest in the roads more widely taken.

Jim's Sino Files: Building on Blacktop

Jiangsu Expressway Co., Ltd.
SHA: 600377, A-shares
Three-year trend: profits up 36.4 percent, revenues up 32.2 percent

In China, you don't have to be the World Bank to get in on the financing of major highways. There are more than twenty toll-road-construction and management companies listed on mainland and Hong Kong exchanges. This company has benefited from the rapid growth of the Jiangsu province, the fertile area around Shanghai with GDP growth 50 percent above the national average. Private car ownership has jumped there by 35 percent a year, too. No wonder expressway fees accounted for 64 percent of revenues.

Zhejiang Expressway Co., Ltd.
HKG: 0576, H-shares
Three-year trend: profits up 37 percent, revenues up 52.1 percent

Also benefits from being in central coastal China, running the popular Shanghai-Hangzhou as well as Hangzhou-Ningbo expressways. They even own the businesses along the way, like gas stations and billboards.

Anhui Expressway Co., Ltd.
SHA: 600012, A-shares; HKG: 0995, H-shares
Three-year trend: profits up 96.9 percent, revenues up 33.6 percent

Anhui operates five toll roads and has been adding lanes in response to the rapid urbanization of Anhui's capital, Hefei (population 4.4 million).

Tianjin Port Development Holdings, Ltd.
SHA: 600717, A-shares; HKG: 3882, H-shares
Three-year trend: profits up 290.8 percent, revenues up 29.6 percent

Tianjin is the major anchorage of northern China, and this is one of the few port management companies that has managed to list overseas.

Shanghai Construction Co., Ltd.
SHA: 600170, A- and B-shares
Three-year trend: profits up 21.6 percent, revenues up 48.3 percent

Need a builder? Shanghai Construction's major projects include the remodeling of Shanghai's Pudong International Airport and Zhonghuanxian Expressway.

The Drive for Four Wheels

Increased demand from a hungry pool of consumers, with prices falling due to volume plus improved efficiency of sales and production: no wonder carmakers want a piece of the China market. But ultimately, China's roads will be claimed by vehicles made by the Chinese themselves. Already, there are more than 130 domestic car companies manufacturing passenger vehicles in China—more than any other country in the world. Many of these companies will not survive the next few years, but I suspect some could emerge as global champions.

For now, foreign carmakers have their strong brand names and reputations to buoy them in the Chinese market. The ordinary Chinese consumers are still suspicious about the quality of their own domestic producers. Identical foreign car models assembled in Japan or Europe or the United States (colloquially called "assembled at place of origin") sell at a premium, compared to those assembled on China's mainland (called "assembled out of place of origin"). Once the Chinese realize their own ability to produce some of the world's finest, most reliable cars, global car brands could very well go topsy-turvy.

There are relatively few global automotive players. The top six—GM, Ford, DaimlerChrysler, Toyota, Honda, and Nissan—account for over 85 percent of the global market. But foreign carmakers that enter the Chinese market are required to team with a domestic firm in ventures with a split of no more than 50-50, and these alliances have thus far been of great benefit to local partners. For instance, Shanghai Automotive has joint ventures with both Volkswagen and General Motors. Shanghai Automotive doesn't care if Volkswagen loses customers to GM or vice versa. It benefits from sales on either side. Meanwhile, it is adopting the technology gleaned from working with both of these global leaders to develop its own strategy.

In June 2006, Shanghai Automotive gave a hint of what's in store for foreign joint-venture partners by announcing that it would raise up to US$2 billion in another initial public offering on the Hong Kong stock exchange. Later that month, Shanghai Automotive announced that it had poached a GM China president, Philip Murtaugh, and had appointed him to oversee overseas manufacturing and operations. A month later, Shanghai Automotive announced plans to spend US$1.7 billion developing its own brand model by 2010, and its short-term plan is to reduce its reliance on both GM and Volkswagen.

Volkswagen once sold three out of ten cars in China, but has seen market share slide to 17 percent in 2006. With two joint ventures, VW sold over 690,000 cars in China in 2006, while next-best General Motors was around 400,000. Both will be more and more reliant on China to stay competitive. Faced with declining profits and growing competition in the United States, GM is rolling out upgraded models under several brand names—and is committing to electric-hybrid cars in China faster than they are in the United States. Honda and Toyota have rushed new lines onto the Chinese market also. Volkswagen estimates it will double the number of cars it builds in China by 2008 to 1.6 million vehicles. So far, a 2007 tax on luxury cars in China, aimed at improving gas mileage, has had little effect—with top officials still willing to spend big for Cadillacs and Buicks.

While the government has tried to keep foreign brands out of China, customs duties have lowered from 50 percent in 2003 to 25 percent in June 2006. That isn't so different from the tariffs in a lot of other Asian countries. And some firms get around this by setting up plants or parts factories on the mainland (though, even these have to export). Still, it is brands we do not yet know that may provide the real leverage for investors. Already, in 2005, domestic carmakers accounted for 27 percent of the Chinese market, but they are aiming for more. The CEO of one Chinese car company has said, "As the Chinese car industry mixes with the global market, how Chinese car companies choose to create core competencies and independent labels is the most important consideration."

China first became a net exporter of cars and trucks in 2006, as exports surged 120 percent over the previous year. This was also the first year a Chinese company, Geely, caused a stir by exhibiting models at the Detroit auto show. The Ministry of Commerce aims to lift vehicle and auto part exports to US$120 billion within ten years. In August 2006, eight cities were designated automobile export zones by the Chinese government and will be given a variety of tax incentives to encourage automobile exporting in those areas. The regions are the coastal ports of Shanghai, Tianjin, Xiamen, and Taizhou, as well as the Yangtze river cities of Wuhan, Wuhu, and Chongqing and northeastern Changchun. These regional companies will provide another means to invest in China's domestic auto industry.

In fact, there is currently overcapacity in automobile manufacturing in China, so it may be better to look for beneficiaries of this trend in auto component companies such as glass and tires, or even motel chains. While the behemoths of the auto world may be ramming head-on into one another, a safer course may be to invest in a burgeoning parts and supply market. Over the decade, Chinese auto parts companies have shifted their reputation in the industry from churning out poor-quality, poorly priced parts to being the highest-quality manufacturers in the world. General Motors even purchased US$200 million in parts made in China in 2005. That year, for the first time, the Chinese started exporting more auto parts than it imports (at a time when the U.S. industry is in shambles and finding it increasingly difficult to compete in China). In 2006, the United States joined the European Union in petitioning the World Trade Organization to overturn a Chinese tariff policy that discourages imports of auto parts.

One reason that the Chinese government has deliberately held off a significant revaluation of the currency is to help support nascent

Chinese industries such as the car industry. When the government decontrols the renminbi and the currency appreciates, imported vehicles will be cheaper for Chinese customers, and demand for foreign cars will rise. But this will also make it easier for Chinese companies to expand through their own foreign acquisitions. The best known, of course, is Nanjing Automobile's takeover of the respected British company Rover. Already, Nanjing has moved assembly lines and jobs back to China, since it hopes to revive the distinguished MG sports cars as made-in-China collectors' items.

China already exports its low-priced compact models to thirty countries, mostly in the developing world. Geely Auto and Chery Auto seem best poised for expansion. Chery may be a conscious copy of Chevy, or a misspelled "cherry," but its plans for expansion are no joke—though their small models have been a hard sell for Americans so far. Some Edsels may be on the way, but so might some future Camrys. And who would have thought Americans would ever be taking their vacations in Korean Kias?

Jim's Sino Files: Auto Pilots

Shanghai Automotive Co., Ltd.
SHA: 600104, A-shares
Three-year trend: profits down 28 percent, revenues up 307.2 percent

China's auto giant, partnering in ventures with GM, VW, and Korea's Ssangyong. In 2006, Shanghai Automotive introduced its own luxury car brand, the Roewe 750 sedan. They have plans to roll out thirty different models by 2010 and eventually export. In 2006, their sales volume rose to 1.34 million vehicles.

Tianjin FAW Xiali Automobile Co., Ltd.
SHE: 000927, A-shares
Three-year trend: profits up 1,032.5 percent, revenues up 46.6 percent

Xiali sold nearly two hundred thousand cars in 2005 and has partnered with Toyota. Its joint-venture Audi A61 vehicle won "2005

China Car of the Year," bestowed by China Central Television. But Xiali also won the "2005 China Independent Brand Car of the Year" for its own Fulixin N3 passenger car. Xiali's CEO has said, "The Fulixin is our first step toward a truly 'Chinese car.' "

Chongqing Changan Automobile Co., Ltd.
SHE: 00625, A-shares; 200625 B-shares
Three-year trend: profits down 50.9 percent, revenues up 38.6 percent

Among other domestic brands you might want to take for a test spin is Changan, Ford Motor's partner in China.

Geely Automobile Holdings Ltd.
HKG: 0175, H-shares; OTC: GELYF
Three-year trend: profits up 164.9 percent, revenues up 298.1 percent

Geely, first to show in Detroit, had hoped to sell cars in the United States by 2008. But crash tests and emissions controls have not been up to snuff. Still, shares have surged well above the Hong Kong index average gain. It is not to be confused with Chery Automobile Co., not yet publicly traded, which exports low-priced cars to many developing nations and has plants in Russia and Iran.

Great Wall Motor Co., Ltd.
HKG: 2333, H-shares; OTC: GWLLF
Three-year trend: profits up 51.5 percent, revenues up 54.4 percent

Great Wall is a market leader in SUV's and pickup trucks, exporting since 2001 to the Middle East and South America.

Wanxiang Qianchao Co., Ltd.
SHE: 000559, A-shares
Three-year trend: profits up 15.2 percent, revenues up 44.7 percent

At last count, there were 4,447 major auto parts producers in China, and Wanxiang is the largest. It began as a repair shop for farm equipment and now ranks as China's third-biggest non-state-owned company. The firm even employs close to a thousand employees in the United States and Europe. To gain access to more customers and better technology, Wanxiang has bought several U.S. companies.

Weichai Power Co., Ltd.
SHE: 000338, A-shares; HKG: 2338, H-shares; OTC: WEICF
Three-year trend: profits up 32.8 percent, revenues up 7.78 percent

Wanxiang's main competitor.

Denway Motors Ltd.
HKG: 0203, H-shares; OTC: DENMF
Three-year trend: profits up 10.1 percent, revenues down 16.8 percent

A major parts supplier.

Another Track

While China embraces the thrills of car cruising in the American manner, it is hardly abandoning a decidedly European-style dedication to its trains. For journeys over sixty miles, railways remain the country's number one option.

British merchants built China's first railway in Shanghai in 1876, and ever since then China's "iron rooster" has pulled all the country's heavy loads, industrial or human. Even when Chairman Mao fomented revolution, he did it from a private train car and got his Red Guards to hop aboard when they liked. Today, fitted with doilies and antimacassars, and plied by porters replenishing hot water thermoses, China's first-class compartments help ease multiday train trips across the country's vast expanses and through winding mountain passes (the western route between Chengdu and Kunming boasts the most tunnels on any line in the world). Even today, I find there's no better way to judge China's progress or its social displacement than to check on the main big-city stations, especially in job-magnets like

Guangzhou and Shanghai. Here, the platforms and terminal approaches have been turned into crowded temporary cities where China's "floating population" pauses to camp, sleep, or wait for a connection. The groups of capped peasants squatting in sooty stations make for one of those unforgettable human spectacles to be glimpsed only in the world's most crowded, and now most restless, land.

In China, over ten billion passenger journeys occur each year. For starters, China has completed two of mankind's most outstanding and miraculous pieces of track. Most recent is the "world's highest," the 1,251-mile link from Qinghai province to Tibet—with over 341 miles of track specially engineered to lie on frozen tundra. Costing US$4.2 billion, it began operating in July 2006. And China plans to extend three more lines through the mountain region, eventually linking with India at its borders. Four thousand passengers a day now ride the new Tibet rail line, which sounds so thrilling it might even get me out of the saddle or driver's seat. Not just an amazing tourist experience, the new line is a transport link that, for better or worse, will speed Tibet's further integration into China's economy. This will likely engender further investment opportunities in the still relatively undeveloped region (though neither of the companies that manage the two train lines is publicly listed).

The other piece of track is the US$1.2 billion German-designed maglev that covers the distance from Shanghai's new Pudong airport to the city subway system at 267 miles per hour and will eventually link to Hangzhou, thirty-five miles away, in fifteen minutes. Generally such "prestige" projects—like America putting a man on the moon— are not solid investments. But you can make a lot of money indirectly through suppliers and contractors who benefit. And more miraculous trains are on the way, with French, German, and Japanese firms bidding for huge contracts to construct "bullet trains" linking major cities like Shanghai and Beijing. Already, the Chinese just put into service high-speed trains of their own construction on twenty-eight major routes.

China is also working to become a major power in maritime transport. China State Shipbuilding Corporation (CSSC) has seen a significant increase in recent years, helping make China third in the world behind Japan and Korea. Established in 1999, CSSC remains state-owned and tied to the military—which, for now, means it is unlisted. The company has benefited from a partnership with America's Foremast Maritime, owned by Chinese American James Chao, father of Bush administration secretary of labor Elaine Chao. CSSC also makes submarines and has entered into partnership to jointly operate new shipyards on the Yangtze River, aimed at increasing the Shanghai area's capacity fourfold.

But trains come first. In 2006, the government announced it will invest US$190 billion, the most in Chinese history, for a massive 20 percent railway expansion by 2010. Eight new lines will link remote areas while intercity express trains will become the rule. At the time of the announcement, Chinese analysts commented that the "railway industry's boom is expected to last over ten years."

Jim's Sino Files: All Aboard

Daqin Railway Co., Ltd.
SHA: 601006, A-shares
Three-year trend: profits up 82.8 percent, revenues up 124.2 percent

Daqin's August 2006 IPO was seventy times oversubscribed—and became the second-largest IPO by a Chinese company, after the Bank of China. Strategic investors like China Life Insurance and the CITIC (among China's oldest and more powerful investment groups) took about 30 percent of the new shares. Headquartered in Shanxi province, Daqin operates the largest coal transportation railway and offers services for coal as well as for coke, cement, iron, steel, and wood.

Guangshen Railway Co., Ltd.
SHA: 601333, A-shares; HKG: 0525; NYSE: GSH, ADR; OTC: GNGYF
Three-year trend: profits up 36.2 percent, revenues up 18.3 percent

One of the most widely listed in the railway industry, Guangshen has a monopoly on lines in the Pearl River Delta from Guangzhou to

Shenzhen (the border with Hong Kong). In 2004, China's Ministry of Railways (which owns two thirds of Guangshen Railway) announced plans to double passenger capacity by constructing a fourth rail line. The ministry also plans to complete a high-speed link between Guangzhou and Zhuhai (a special economic zone bordering Macau) and an expansion of links to Wuhan (a megalopolis on the Yangtze River). The continued easing of travel restrictions between mainland China and Hong Kong means further opportunity for Guangshen.

China Railway Erju Co., Ltd.
SHA: 600528, A-shares
Three-year trend: profits up 44.2 percent, revenues up 105.4 percent

In 2005, this company, which builds everything from bridges to tunnels, took on a mere 147 projects and they have recently signed a strategic agreement to work on financing with Lehman Brothers.

Also of note, China Railway Construction Corp., a Fortune Global 500 company, has announced plans to list shares in Hong Kong and Shanghai, which may be complete by the time this publishes. The state-owned company had US$15 billion in revenue in 2005 and should benefit especially from the government's ambitious rail expansion.

China COSCO Holdings Co., Ltd.
SHA: 601919, A-shares; HKG: 1919, H-shares
Three-year trend: profits down 36.1 percent, revenues up 58.4 percent

Owns more than six hundred Chinese-flag merchant ships, but profits have fallen due to fuel costs and other factors.

On the eve of the founding of Communist China in 1949, the country had opened over sixty-eight hundred miles of railways, and by 1997, the nation's total railway track was six times higher. Now, it seems, that was just a first stage. By all means possible, China is on the move.

6

Tourism: Up, Up, and Away

As I write this, the first Chinese tour group to Antarctica is in the midst of its journey. A daring travel agency in the southern city of Guangzhou—where people never see any snow—is charging US$10,000 a head for the trip. I wonder whether they're taking along chopsticks and just what the penguins are going to think. The trip is being staged from the top of Argentina, as a celebration of that country's ascension to the Chinese government's list of "approved destinations" for its citizens. Since 2001, the number of countries that offer streamlined tourist visas in a reciprocal manner with China has risen from a measly 18 to an astounding 132.

Having traipsed through most of those lands on my two round-the-world journeys, I can appreciate the natural urge to explore our planet. Call me a serial wanderer. Not everybody has to put in 152,000 miles on one vacation, but hitting the road is more than a universal right. It's a universal urge to "see what we've never seen and taste what we've never tasted," as one old Chinese man put it. And that's been pent up inside more than a billion people who've only recently been able to indulge their wanderlust.

Travel, both foreign and domestic, is expanding the frontiers of

Chinese enterprise—making this an area for investment worth more than just quick sightseeing. I'd say that it's a pretty safe bet that Chinese tourists will soon be found in every place worth going on earth, and in large enough numbers to transform an industry that already accounts for 9 percent of global employment and 11 percent of global GDP.

When it comes to domestic tourism, earnings there have risen faster than China's overall GDP for the past quarter century. In 2005, it was estimated that China's domestic tourism provides employment to 77.6 million people and created 4.3 percent of the country's revenue that year. The number of travelers just within China itself rose 15 percent in 2006 to 1.39 billion, with revenues for the entire tourism industry up 17.9 percent in the same year.

Back when I started touring China, it seemed I was doing it nearly solo. Magnificent caves, desert vistas, and ancient fortresses along the Great Wall were mine to enjoy in peace. The many hilltop temples and religious sites of China were still spooky places. Now I have to elbow my way into Buddhist, Taoist, and Confucianist sites of worship, through crowds of sightseers thick as the clouds of incense. Some of China's "holy Buddhist mountains" are now publicly listed stocks.

What excites me most is the relative youth of the industry. Again, think along the lines of the United States around the time the first decent highways were built and the concept of motels or Holiday Inns came into fashion. Or think of Germany and Japan after the Second World War once the people there had recovered their resources enough to start seeing the world in a better way. Along with agriculture and water resources, travel—both foreign and especially domestic—could be one of the most "recession-proof" areas for investment. And once stocks can weather bad times, they get talked up even more.

Talk about taking off: a Goldman Sachs study projects an annual 17 percent increase in the number of China's domestic tourists for each of the next eight years. And when it comes to heading overseas, it's fair to say that only a trickle of those 1.3 billion have yet to get their passports stamped.

The Occidental Tourists

One common joke in China tells about the omnivorous Cantonese going to African game parks and salivating over every animal they were supposed to be preserving with mutters of "Tastes good, tastes good. . . ." Pretty soon we're all going to know exactly what it is like to go on a "safari with Chinese characteristics."

If you want to see the biggest change in travel since the invention of the jet airplane, you need look no farther than a few hundred yards from the birthplace of Marco Polo in Venice. Barely two cobblestone alleys and one canal away from where Europe's first chronicler of China was reared, there's a restaurant hung with red lanterns. Il Tempio del Paradiso is one of thirty to forty restaurants serving Chinese-style ravioli to curious Asians invading the city on water. Like the Japanese before them, groups from mainland China are the ones being serenaded in flotillas of overpriced Venetian gondolas.

It was similar conditions—higher spending power, a stronger currency, and, especially, shorter working hours—that propelled the Japanese to storm the Louvre and the pyramids with their Nikons back in the 1980s. And soon the Japanese wave is going to look like a trickle. After all, there are 125 million Japanese to 1.3 billion Chinese—over ten times as many souvenir seekers. And even if many are still too poor to spend on excursions, there will be more added to the pool of millions by the day.

Go to Bali, Rio, or London's West End not too long from now, and you'll see foot massage shops and gold jewelers—plus directions in Chinese, status items aimed at Chinese consumers, slews of Chinese-speaking guides. Look for museums to start tagging their master-pieces with pictographs. Chinese-language channels will be beamed into every five-star hotel, and probably most of the five-roach ones, too. A big trend now is that the Chinese, always sports-minded and health-conscious, are discovering skiing with a vengeance. From an estimated two hundred skiers in 1999, there are now over two hundred ski areas—far northern Heilongjiang has a premier resort, helped with an initial US$150 million investment from the government. Look for China's northern provinces, and even Russia's far east, to benefit. Naturally, the cooped-up Chinese are going to be seeking even more of those wide-open spaces.

It's tough to come by accurate statistics on this Chinese mass migration (on the decks of cruise ships, not in the holds of freighters). That's because the most accessible and popular territories of Hong Kong and Macau, returned to China as Special Administrative Regions in 1997 and 1999, respectively, are counted as "foreign" destinations. And there's no way to keep track of how many Chinese move on to secondary destinations from there. One study estimates that only six million of the thirty million outbound Chinese in 2005 went beyond the two enclaves on the South China Sea. Still, the total of outbound tourists rose by 11.22 percent to 34.52 million in 2006, and those headed abroad had already increased 250 percent in the previous five years. The United Nations World Tourism Organization predicts that by 2020, Chinese tourists will be fourth in the world in the number of foreign trips. Barring some unforeseen border-closing calamity, the Chinese will be number one by 2035. Within the next few years, China's travel and tourism industry taken as a whole will be second only to that in the United States. And all of this is happening quicker than you can say "Hyatt Hotel."

That the Chinese should be bitten so hard by the travel bug is no surprise. They were pretty much pinned down by wars, catastrophes, and economic collapse as modern mass travel evolved. After the Communist regime took power in 1949, journeys were so strictly controlled that an average citizen could never even dream about getting their hands on that rare artifact known as a passport. Only high officials, or those who curried their favor, ever got a peek at foreign lands. Even at the start of the reforms in the 1980s, the government did little to stimulate the travel industry—worrying that educated citizens would escape on one-way trips to the West. At first, only watchful state-designated agencies could sell tickets to invited groups.

On his first trip to China, U.S. president Ronald Reagan is said to have lectured Chinese senior leader Deng Xiaoping about free travel as a basic human right, urging him to loosen restrictions as a goodwill gesture. According to this urban legend, the wily Deng surprised Reagan with the comeback, "Okay, I'll do that. Now how many Chinese do you want in California? Ten million? Fifty million? A hundred million?"

Soon enough, those hundred million will be finding their way to Saint-Tropez, Spain's Costa Brava, or Australia's Gold Coast. And that means benefits not merely for travel agents, online booking sites, airlines, or railways, but for hotel and restaurant chains, spas and beach resorts, amusement parks and special attractions, related activities from skiing to shopping, even manufacturers of motion sickness pills, suntan lotion, luggage, backpacks, and, as some studies have cited, cosmetics instead of postcards. A recent study showed 60 percent of Chinese ramblers are women, 65 percent of whom are under forty-five, and are spending an average of US$546 per jaunt. And each is now allowed to carry and exchange up to US$20,000—the limit was first set at US$2,000. In June 2006, *The Economist* reported that Chinese tourists spent more on shopping, per day and per trip, than travelers from Europe, Japan, or America.

Most still stay relatively close to home, with Asian countries and regions accounting for 90.4 percent of Chinese outbound travel as of November 2005. Japan, Thailand, Singapore, and Malaysia were among the top draws, while a whopping 70 percent journeyed no farther than Hong Kong and Macau. The Chinese government started allowing group trips to those two destinations as early as 1983, and ten years later instituted the "individual travel scheme" (ITS)—allowing citizens in neighboring Guangdong province, as well as Shanghai and Beijing, to obtain travel permits for the two enticing enclaves in less time and for far less expense than getting a passport. Today, the scheme covers thirty-four cities and 200 million mainland residents, with plans to expand to some 535 million people the privilege of traveling for "personal reasons."

Those reasons are pretty obvious. Hong Kong, as a British possession, had long ago evolved into China's freewheeling window on the West, an entrepôt whose main reason for being was its tax-free exchange of trade. Aside from sampling the splendors of its fresh seafood, the main reason for mainland Chinese going there is to open their wallets. For the time being anyway, Louis Vuitton purses or high-end perfumes are between 10 and 50 percent lower-priced than across the China border, and there is still more to choose from in Hong Kong's self-consciously snobbish malls for the estimated fifty million Chinese—and growing—who are potential customers for luxury goods. In anticipation of the day when Hong Kong no longer holds any retail advantage over Shanghai, its civic leaders have wisely moved to create Hong Kong Disneyland, which opened as the first on Chinese soil in late 2005. (But look out—Shanghai has already approached Disney officials about their own franchise, though it would not open until at least 2010.)

Macau's appeal is even more one-dimensional. Though full of wondrous architectural and cultural remnants of its five-hundred-plus-year history in Portuguese hands as Asia's first and last colony, Macau's main source of revenue has long been its gambling casinos—traditionally frequented by Hong Kongers making the one-hour ferry ride over, and once monopolized by Stanley Ho's Macao Gaming Company (no public listing). But Macau's return to the motherland on December 20, 1999, signaled the start of serious gaming on a scale never previously imagined. When the Portuguese agreed to return Macau to China in the Sino-Portuguese Joint Declaration of 1987, the treaty stipulated that Macau could retain a unique lifestyle and special privileges unavailable elsewhere in China, most important among them legalized gambling. As Macau has become more the province of Chinese tourists—over one billion people live within a three-hour plane ride—so its casinos have grown at 22 percent annually through 2005. That same year, the gaming take accounted for 70 percent of Macau's revenue.

Today, giant players have entered the competition to cash in on Macau's transformation into the Asian Las Vegas. The first phase of a US$13 billion project on a stretch of reclaimed land known as the Cotai Strip opened in 2007 and features seven resort hotel casinos and more than ten thousand guest rooms. The principle operator and beneficiary of Cotai is the Las Vegas Sands Corporation, which previously opened the Sands Macao as the first Western-operated casino in 2004, all 163,000 smoke-clogged square feet. Sands will be opening its own version of the Venetian hotel from Las Vegas, and Wynn Macau, operated by Wynn Resorts, already opened its gilded doors in September 2006. The new kid on the block is aiming for even higher luxury, betting that Chinese gamblers will become increasingly sophisticated and even family-oriented.

Stakes are high because Chinese gamble away far more than any other of the world's high rollers. According to the investment bank UBS, 18.7 million people visited Macau in 2005, compared to 38.6 million for Las Vegas, and the average daily take at Macau's tables was US$12,000, compared to just US$2,600 in Las Vegas. Gross gaming revenues in Macau reached US$3.1 billion in the first half of 2006, compared to the Las Vegas Strip, which made US$3.3 billion in that same period.

Now even staid Singapore, already a popular destination for Chinese due to its sedate cleanliness, tropical climate, and shared Chinese heritage, is being tempted by such a bonanza. In April 2005, Singapore lifted a four-decade ban on casinos, despite strong local opposition. Two casinos, the Marina Bay and the Sentosa, are set to open in 2009.

With few tropics of their own, the Chinese are hungry for sun and sand. Many Chinese are on their first hard-earned explorations—42 percent, says one estimate—the equivalent of those working-class Englishmen who party on Spain's cut-rate beaches. This has led to the scourge of "zero-sum tourism"—air and hotel packages actually sold at a loss in places like Thailand, where agents try to recoup their money through commissions at shops selling gems, carved trinkets, and especially popular herbal aphrodisiacs including Thai crocodile meat. But "zero sum" is not a point at which China's zillions will be staying for long.

With India's incredible wealth of culture and scenery, and with more convenient links growing between the countries as they become friendlier, the other Asian giant should eventually become another beneficiary of China's travel boom in the years ahead. India is both close and cheap, so tourists from both countries will be flooding the other. Indian tourism companies such as India Hospitality Corporation (LSE [London Stock Exchange]: IHC) may benefit.

But neither nearby Taiwan nor the United States have yet been given "approved destination status" by the Chinese. And that means both could see a huge boom once visa hurdles are lowered.

America is called "the beautiful country" in Chinese. Waves of immigrants have cemented historic ties between the two countries across the Pacific. The famed sights of the United States have near-mythic status to most Chinese—including the Golden Gate Bridge, the Grand Canyon, and the Empire State Building. Due to the appeal of gambling, Las Vegas is almost always included on the first-time itinerary. Chinese also like to see the famed universities, perhaps checking out where to send the kids, including Stanford and especially Yale (where the first Chinese to graduate from an American university was named Yung Wing, class of 1854).

Yet, ever since 9/11, the numbers of Chinese tourists has been decreasing due to stringent and suspicious visa procedures. Many American travel industry groups are lobbying for changes in policy before they miss out on a huge market. China has expressed interest in granting the United States approved destination status, but the United States has not responded. Ironically, as China supplants the United States as a destination of choice, the best way to pump up the number of tourists to the United States would be to allow in more Chinese tourists.

Taiwan has even more obvious appeal. More and more Chinese are headed there, braving the hassle of long, indirect flights so they can size up the "wayward province," try different styles of Chinese food and hot springs, or see long-separated relatives. A survey of Taiwan tour operators in August 2005 revealed they expected a growth of 20 to 60 percent as soon as they could be fully open to mainland traffic.

Increasingly, the Chinese are headed farther afield. The United Kingdom was granted approved destination status only in 2005 and a group of eighty senior citizens headed off the very first day on Virgin Atlantic Airways for a seven-night tour. They even got to dine with Britain's Prince Andrew. The number of Chinese visitors to the UK has doubled since 2000 to more than a hundred thousand a year, and is expected to rise 15 to 20 percent per year through 2015.

As the Chinese renminbi strengthens, overseas travel will become increasingly cheaper for Chinese citizens. Not only will they be exploring farther afield, but they will be bringing more and more money with them. Since the Chinese government changed the laws to allow every citizen to take US$20,000 out of China annually, travel spending has boomed. Tastes and demands will get more sophisticated—there's already an increasing market for long-stay serviced apartments for Chinese around Asia—and you'll hear fewer complaints about penny-pinchers who never get off the tour bus.

Better load up on shares of luggage manufacturers, too. The Chinese are just starting to pack their bags.

Jim's Sino Files: Voyager Missions

Ctrip.com International, Ltd.
NASDAQ: CTRP, ADR
Three-year trend: profits up 80.7 percent, revenues up 132.8 percent

and

eLong, Inc.
NASDAQ: LONG, ADR
Three-year trend: profits US$1.11 million up from US$18.38 million loss, revenues up 91.1 percent

Both companies were founded in 1999 and are available in ADR's. These popular online travel service providers search the best data on hotels and flights to domestic destinations as well as foreign destinations. Like Travelocity, these discount consolidators generate revenue through commissions, targeting the individual leisure or business traveler. Expedia has a 52 percent share in eLong. Ctrip's stock prices have been uneven, surprising for a company that has English interface as well.

China CYTS Tours Holding Co., Ltd.
SHA: 600138, A-shares
Three-year trend: profits up 26.1 percent, revenues up 64.2 percent

CYTS (China Youth Travel Service) became the first travel service listed on the stock exchange back in 1997. A brick-and-mortar travel agency with online operations as well, CYTS is affiliated with the older state-run CITS, the only travel agency among China's top five hundred companies, but unlisted. The two companies handled tickets and arrangements for close to half a million clients in 2005, whether inbound, outbound, or group tours.

Shanghai Jinjiang International Travel Co., Ltd.
SHA: 900929, B-shares

Three-year trend: profits down 47.2 percent, revenues up 33.4 percent

Another ticketing agency, Shanghai Jinjiang has diversified into such fields as interior design and freight forwarding.

TravelSky Technology Ltd.
HKG: 0696, H-shares; OTC: TSYHF

Three-year trend: profits up 15.3 percent, revenues up 33.4 percent

An IT service provider that caters to the tourism boom. Formed in 2000 by twenty-one Chinese airlines, the company develops software products and services for airport passenger processing and develops air-cargo-system e-commerce platforms for airlines, airports, travel service providers, travel agencies, and corporations. In 2005, the company's Electronic Travel Distribution system processed more than 151.4 million passenger bookings on domestic and overseas commercial airlines, representing an increase of 14.5 percent over 2004.

Las Vegas Sands Corporation
NYSE: LVS

Three-year trend: profits down 10.7 percent, revenues up 86.9 percent

An American firm with much of its future growth bound up in China. Its Macau investments are clearly the main driver behind its stock price, which has more than doubled in the past five years. That was before its Macau Venetian became fully operational—and the company is still awaiting permission to transform a tiny island off Macau, technically part of the Chinese city of Zhuhai, into an even bigger gambling enclave. Such prestigious names as Four Seasons (NYSE: FS), Shangri-La (HKG: 0069, H-shares), and Hilton (NYSE: HLN) also have properties in the new Cotai Strip mega-casino.

Far Eastern Air Transport Corp.
TPE: 5605
Three-year trend: profits down 400 percent, revenues up 8.8 percent

Every time rumors circulate about initiating direct flights, as in June 2005, Taipei-listed stocks related to Taiwanese tourism immediately rally. In 2003, this Taiwanese airline saw share prices jump 10 percent when direct chartered flights were authorized.

No Place Like Home

When locals welcomed Marco Polo to the desert oasis of Hami, they offered him his choice of all their wives. No such luck for me on my first arrival. Trying my best to "sack out" in the town's single fleabag hotel, I noticed that my pillow seemed especially hard. Examining it closely, I saw that I was laying my head on a full sack of rice.

Just fifteen years back, China's "hospitality industry," if you dared call it that, didn't hand out individual hotel keys. A set of hostesses with the demeanor of nasty nurses making ward rounds surveyed the hallways and let you into your room when absolutely necessary. But they always had access, to keep an eye on foreign devils or to keep replenishing the boiled drinking water in thermoses. The handful of luxury hotels, like Beijing's Great Wall Sheraton, were as much showcases of the Western lifestyle as they were rare refuges for travelers weary of sullen socialist-style service. No matter what I asked for, the most common phrase, the first Chinese words heard by visitors, was

"Mei you." Pronounced "mayo," this could mean "There is none," "We're out of that," "No way," or "Forget it."

Today, China has rejoined the Asian mainstream in terms of courtesy, hospitality, and downright overeagerness to please the guest. The Chinese have not learned to bow as much as to take bows (and enjoy the rewards) when jobs are done well. And Westerners are a conspicuous minority, as ever more opulent establishments are being created largely for upscale Chinese traffic.

Not so long ago, either, you couldn't purchase a round-trip plane ticket in China. Locals and foreigners alike had to spend whole days shoving their way to the front of counters to get a seat going to some province, then do the same thing to get back. Many of China's roads were off-limits to foreigners, and nearly as impassable for the few local motorists. Today, an extensive network of modern airlines, highways, and accommodations serve vast numbers who have just obtained their first disposable income and first car. While the trend may be less visible than glitzy Macau casinos, the huge upsurge of travel within China itself is filling even more hotel rooms and pockets.

Again, some of the numbers tossed around may be misleading. The Chinese government considers a journey of more than six hours, no matter the reason, as "travel," and one estimate has it that 80 percent of Chinese still spend no more than an average of US$15 per trip. But all told, income from China's tourism industry was projected to pass the one trillion mark (in Chinese yuan—still a hefty US$130 billion) in 2007.

Top leaders like Vice Premier Wu Yi have been exhorting this burgeoning sector to play an even more significant role in "expanding domestic consumption." In 2006, the world's highest passenger train route opened up Tibet as never before. Distant attractions, like the old town of Lijiang, a UNESCO World Heritage site set in the mountainous area of northern Kunming that first inspired the term "Shangri-La," aren't just accessible now, but are downright overdeveloped and overrun. In the decade from 1991 onward, tourist arrivals in Lijiang, for instance, rose from 198,000 to 3,270,000. And, with over half the populace now dependent on travelers instead of farming, average income also rose from US$60 a year to over US$650.

Another government estimate put the number of urbanites heading out for fresh air and recreation in China's as yet underexploited countryside at three hundred million. And the cities have not been neglected, either. With every Chinese bent on seeing Tiananmen Square and other national monuments, Beijing received 132 million visitors in 2006, up 14 percent from the previous year. The 2008 Olympics is sure to increase that number. And Shanghai attracted ninety million.

All this is in a country where mobility is a relatively new concept. Under the Maoist model, social order was held in place by forced employment and fixed residence. People were forbidden to travel beyond cities where they were registered, and checking into a hotel, even obtaining food, could require permission letters. Hospitality was determined by rank, and as recently as 1991, one's class of train ticket was determined by one's position. Perhaps the only example of mass tourism during the first forty years of the People's Republic was the brief period when zealous young Red Guards were encouraged to ride railways around the country for free, not to experience first or second class, but to foment "class struggle."

Now everybody takes off on three long national holidays purposely instituted by the government in 1999 to encourage and stimulate travel. These so-called golden weeks, for Chinese New Year, May Day (now "Labor Day"), and the anniversary every October of the founding of the People's Republic, are a mad scramble where everyone heads for ancestral homes or tourist attractions, all at the same time. An estimated three hundred million were on the move in 2006, with twenty-nine million visiting tourist sites in a single day. On the first day of the 2005 May holiday, three million people took air flights.

While travel agents and scenic destinations are reaping huge profits, some government officials are so concerned with the overload on national transport that they are talking about spreading holidays to other traditional festivals like Qingming, when Chinese visit the graves of their ancestors. Eventually, the Chinese will relieve the madness of moving all at once—to the greater benefit of travelers and the travel industry. According to the China National Tourism Administration, 92.2 million people traveled during the seven-day break in February 2006, an increase of 17.7 percent.

The Chinese have rediscovered their own heritage with a vengeance, packing the kung fu shows at the famed Shaolin Temple and packing even more the Nanjing mausoleum of the father of modern China, Sun Yat-sen—visited far more by Chinese than foreigners. Where there was hardly a place to buy a soda or a souvenir, whole townships of hawkers have sprung up. Plans for sprucing up Beijing's attractions for the Olympics include moving vendors and touts away from the Great Wall for the first time, and adding wheelchair access and better English signage to every place from the Ming Tombs to the Summer Palace.

This doesn't mean "foreign guests" are being neglected—or thrown out of their seats. Maybe it's the nation's new image as an economic marvel, the appeal of historic cities or kung fu temples, or just improved facilities, but in 2004, the Middle Kingdom passed fabled Italy for fourth place in terms of inbound arrivals. If Hong Kong numbers were added, China would be number two. Earnings of US$35.5 billion through tourism placed China sixth in the world. And that represents over a hundredfold increase since 1978, when people entering the country were more likely to be viewed as spies. Again, the U.N. World Tourism Organization estimates that China—helped by "overseas compatriots" from Hong Kong, Macau, and Taiwan—will be the world's number one destination before 2020.

Of course, all of this is great news for taxi drivers, bilingual tour guides (in huge demand now), and travel agencies—and a significant reduction in the hurdles to becoming licensed, as mandated by the WTO, should provide an opportunity for more overseas operators to do business in China. Slews of new private cooking and hotelier schools are packed with peasants' kids who view this as their best chance to enter a secure profession.

Rice sack pillows notwithstanding, familiar foreign brands have dominated the hospitality sector from the outset. But it now looks like these foreign hotel chains were merely positioning themselves for the real growth to come. And the neglected budget market is where to expect full occupancy. There's still a huge opening here, in a market that saw its first government regulation only as recently as 2002. And what about business traffic in China's one hundred secondary cities, many with a population of two million or more? Among the 11,180 starred hotels registered in the country in 2005, only 14.5 percent were managed by chains, compared to 80 percent in the United States.

Of the estimated 260,000 hotels total, about 60,000 with approximately three million rooms are ranked as "budget" facilities by the National Tourism Administration. I wish America's Best Value Inn, Best Western, and even Howard Johnson had been around in 1984, when five-roach hotels were more the rule. All are on their way to China, and not by slow boat.

Guests on a budget have to eat, too—and show off to business colleagues around the table. As a result, cities like Nanjing have instituted fines for over-ordering, based on the weight of leftover dishes, in order to curb flagrant food waste. That's quite a change from the days of my first forays—when it was hard to find any restaurants at all. And those were barely open more than a few hours a day. You took your life, or stomach, in your hand, crossing floors littered with stray chicken bones, to take your spot hopefully before threadbare tablecloths crisscrossed by folds of dust.

By now, cities like Beijing are said to have as many as one hundred thousand restaurants. But who's counting? In remote outposts like Sichuan's Chengdu, entrepreneurs are falling over one another to open block-long eating palaces—intimate dining for ten thousand, bring earplugs—that feature Chinese-style treatments of newfangled ingredients like lobster, saffron, and caviar. Once they've got a bit of a name, these operators open a string of similar franchises up and down wealthier coastal cities. One of many successful chains, South Beauty, served upscale Sichuan fare beside indoor ponds with stepping-stones to reach private dining tents. Their fare has been featured on airlines, and they plan to expand to New York and have already announced plans for an IPO. Surprisingly, ten such food empires accounted for almost half the share of an all-time high in restaurant earnings in 2005. Most are quick-serve dumpling houses that have spread like hotcakes, but the leader, founded in Inner Mongolia in 1999, is Little Sheep. You can guess the menu—lamb, and lots of it—at their seven-hundred-plus outlets.

Ambitious new theme parks, zoos, spas and resorts, malls, and museums are also multiplying at breakneck pace. (A Fujian amusement park was recently shut down for offering bogus "prizes" that amounted to US$35,000 per ring toss.) There are too many activities allied with tourist traffic for me to list fully. I'll just mention one that could not be more emblematic of the new, capitalist China: golf. This sport allied with rich gentlemen and their private clubs is drawing new adherents, even addicts, so quickly that the Chinese have come to term it "green opium." Since the first course, Chung Shan Hot Spring, was built in 1984 with no earth movers or other equipment, China now has over two hundred courses, making it fifth in the world already, with 20 percent more projected per year. Panicked local governments are actually trying to curb the boom by restricting land use. Whether they think it is good for business or good for health, young people are heading to courses and schools in droves. Even sales for golf clubs increased 25 percent in 2005. And China already boasts the largest golf layout on earth, Shenzhen's astounding Mission Hills with its 216 holes.

When it comes to tourism stocks in China, maybe the best idea is a package deal.

Jim's Sino Files: Leaving the Lantern On

Shanghai Jinjiang International Hotels Development Co., Ltd.
SHA: 900934, A-shares; 600754, B-shares. HKG: 2006, H-shares
Three-year trend: profits up 49.3 percent, revenues up 7.6 percent

This venerable group runs more than 150 hotels nationwide. It has formed a working alliance with Expedia, and its Hong Kong IPO in late 2006 raised US$2.4 billion for renovation of the historic Peace Hotel and many other Jinjiang properties. They have nearly doubled their room capacity in each of the past three years.

Home Inns & Hotels Management Inc.
NASDAQ: HMIN, ADR
Three-year trend: profits up 685.4 percent, revenues up 510 percent

An example of how quickly China's tourism industry is booming. Started by Ctrip cofounder Ji Qi in 2002, Home Inn ran four budget hotels in Beijing, but in May 2007 boasted 145 outlets in forty-one cities. Its business model includes leasing to franchisees. Its share price jumped 59.4 percent in the first day's trading.

Motel 168 hardly sounds Chinese—in fact, it's the first local chain with an English moniker. But this as yet unlisted enterprise, owned by as yet unlisted Shanghai Meilinge Co., is going aggressively for the vastly expanding cut-rate stay market. Top Star, another brash new-comer as yet privately held, vows to open one thousand outlets by 2015.

With the Olympics and other stimuli in mind, the InterContinental Hotels Group (NYSE: IHG), one of the world's oldest hoteliers, with over fifty hotels already in China (including a commitment to manage the luxury hotel at the Beijing Olympics' main site), plans to have over seventy more by 2008, including their Crowne Plaza brand. Marriott (NYSE: MAR) plans to go from thirty-five to one hundred by 2010, and French-based Accor (EPA: AC; OTC: ACRFF) has deemed China its most important market, developing thirty for now.

Beijing Capital Tourism Co., Ltd.
SHA: 600258, A-shares
Three-year trend: profits up 30.6 percent, revenues up 8.3 percent

This company owns two four-star hotels: Beijing Minzu Hotel and Jinglun Hotel in Beijing, expected to benefit from the Beijing Olympics. But it also runs resorts on tropical Hainan Island, and its own travel agencies.

Emei Shan Tourism Co., Ltd.
SHE: 000888, A-shares
Three-year trend: profits down 10.1 percent, revenues up 30.5 percent

This is the concession at the much beloved site in Sichuan that is one of China's five holiest mountains. Pilgrims take days to make the trek here, with help from porters and food sellers, stopping to take in magnificent fog-cloaked views from temple sanctuaries. The company has the monopoly over sales of entrance tickets to the cable cars, plus a hotel and tourism agency.

Huangshan Tourism Development Co., Ltd.
SHA: 600054, A-shares; 900942, B-shares
Three-year trend: profits up 107 percent, revenues up 54.1 percent

This company similarly manages China's even more fabled Yellow Mountain in Anhui province. You might have seen its steep limestone crags and amazing views in Chinese landscape paintings or in the movie *Crouching Tiger, Hidden Dragon*. One note of caution for these cash cows that monopolize popular sites: new regulations will limit ticket price increases to 35 percent over the next three years.

Guilin Tourism Corporation Ltd.
SHE: 000978, A-shares
Three-year trend: profits up 21.6 percent, revenues up 22.2 percent

Holds a similar concession over famed rides down the southwestern Li River through karst formations, a must-see for Chinese and foreign tourists.

Tibet Shengdi Co., Ltd.
SHA: 600749, A-shares
Three-year trend: profits down 2.6 percent, revenues up 15.1 percent

This is the only listed tourism company in Tibet. The company offers tourism site development, tour packages, hotel services, and export of mineral water. With the opening of Qinghai-Tibet railway in mid-2006, Tibet has received a record number of tourists, from which Tibet Shengdi should benefit.

The Jet Set with Chinese Characteristics

When I first got to China, everyone liked to say that the initials of CAAC (the Civil Aviation Administration of China), the state-run air monopoly, stood for "Chinese Airlines Always Crash." Now the company is diversified and the sick joke is very much out-of-date. In fact, overdue consolidation and privatization, increasingly efficient fleets, and ever-increasing passenger traffic are making China's aviation industry look healthy indeed and quite protected from all sorts of crashes.

I am generally bullish on airlines, and that certainly includes China. After all, the worldwide industry lost billions between 2000 and 2006, with at least five major companies worldwide reorganizing or filing for bankruptcy. If that's not a sign of a bottom, I don't know what is. And nobody is going to be caught unaware of fluctuations in fuel prices anymore. Everybody knows about the problems of Airbus, and with Boeing already sold out, supplying a next generation of fleets will be restrained. Airports themselves need to keep up with the growth, too. But there should be five good years on the horizon, probably more in a Chinese market that is still ramping up to head down the runway.

Simply put, China's airline industry is the fastest-growing in the world. It wasn't until 1980 that the government began allowing the establishment of independently run airlines as we know them. China Southwest Airlines, the first of CAAC's six core carriers, was inaugurated in 1987. And Air China, the national carrier, was formed in 1988. But the industry was mired in huge losses caused by rising oil costs and general inefficiency. That was before the restructuring in 2004, when CAAC decided to break into three major groups: Air China, China Eastern, and China Southern. These currently account for more than half of all passengers served. At the time, six non-

CAAC carriers also formed the China Sky Aviation Enterprises Group. These had around one thousand aircraft handling around five hundred routes—but by last year, several key players had defected to merge with the dominant CAAC group.

Now every aircraft manufacturer and aviation supplier is scrambling to fill Chinese sales orders. Boeing, for instance, assembles up to a third of its fleet parts in China already, and was greatly buoyed by a 2005 order from six Chinese carriers for 60 of Boeing's advanced 787 planes to be in service by the time of the Olympics. Commerce Minister Bo Xilai said in 2006 that China will need another 2,000 aircraft by 2020 to service a market set to become three times larger than the U.S. market. CAAC estimates that Chinese airlines will add 100 to 150 aircrafts each year for the next five years. And China won't just be buyers for long. Top officials have announced that the government is making a top priority of building a wide-bodied jet carrier in China within fifteen years.

But the main question facing Chinese airlines is whether they will be able to utilize the added capacity efficiently. They need to train a record number of pilots in record time. In addition, there's a glaring need for more short-distance flights and planes. While aircraft with seventy seats or less account for more than 38 percent of the U.S. market, they are only 9.8 percent in China. Smaller regional airports handle only 6 percent of passengers in China thus far.

Even airports themselves are being upgraded, with Beijing leading the way with an expansion geared to the Olympics as well. A 2004 press release from the airport illustrates the pace of change: "It took 33 years for Beijing Airport's annual passenger volume to increase from zero to 10 million, 7 years to increase from 10 million to 20 million, and only less than 4 years to increase from 20 million to 30 million." By 2006, they exceeded forty million. And like most other airports in Asia, China's new airports are putting the rest of the world to shame. Take a look at New York's Kennedy and LaGuardia if you have to pass through, as I do, and you'll see shabby, overcrowded, inefficient third world facilities. Some baggage claim floors don't even have toilets. It's downright embarrassing compared with China jet ways that are shining virtual cities, complete with high-end malls, healing centers, and in-house hotels.

If you want to see just how far China's faith in its stock markets has come, consider the number of airport terminal authorities that can be found on the board. Every entity, it seems, aspires to the prestige and working capital that comes with an exchange listing. Airports themselves may be a fine way to invest in aviation expansion without risking the expected turbulence of potential mergers and alliances.

All this began with American help. In 1929, Curtiss-Wright, then the largest aviation company in the United States, joined the Chinese government in establishing the China National Aviation Corporation (CNAC). Soon enough, though, disputes with China's nationalist leader Chiang Kai-shek led Curtiss-Wright to sell CNAC to Pan Am. During the Second World War, CNAC pioneered dangerous supply routes between India and China—when the Japanese prevented supplies from getting through the infamous Burma Road. CNAC crews made more than thirty-eight thousand trips over the Himalaya Mountains, transporting vital materials and working alongside the famed American unit known as the Flying Tigers. When the People's Republic was established, Pan Am was forced to sell its remaining stake in CNAC, which was subsumed into the infamous CAAC when it was established in 1949.

Today's Air China wants further consolidation in order to compete with giant international rivals—who are fighting over new Chinese routes, just as Chinese carriers with names we hardly know yet, like China Northern, will be calling more frequently at international destinations. In the aftermath of the September 11 attacks, China proved it had come of age in world aviation by seamlessly aiding international carriers in rerouting flights from war zones in Afghanistan.

There was a spate of accidents on regional Chinese carriers between 1999 and 2001, but since the upgrading that followed, there have been few incidents. And despite the old jokes, national flagship Air China has a good safety record.

Jim's Sino Files: Ways to Take Flight

Air China Ltd.
SHA: 601111, A-shares; HKG: 0753, H-shares; OTC: AICAF, AIRYY
Three-year trend: profits up 24.6 percent, revenues up 34.9 percent

Air China is the national carrier and the official partner for the 2008 Beijing Olympics. In 2006 it struck a HK$8.2 billion deal with Cathy Pacific, selling its stake in Dragon Air (and access to coveted mainland routes) in return for 17.5 percent of the shares in Cathy Pacific (and its international network, as well as reciprocal sales representation). Air China also joined Star Alliance to help boost its international sector.

China Eastern Airlines Co., Ltd.
SHA: 600115, A-shares; HKG: 0670, H-shares; NYSE: CEA, ADR
Three-year trend: US$336.4 million loss down from US$66.8 million profits, revenues up 85 percent

Based in Shanghai, China Eastern might be the biggest airline in the world that you have never heard of. It's the third-largest airline in China in terms of revenue and had more than a 49 percent increase in flyers in 2006—though profits were hard hit by higher oil prices, a crash, and management changes. However, they are going to be converting all of their remaining state-held, tradable shares as part of selling a 20 percent share to Singapore Airlines. The Shanghai World's Fair 2010 won't hurt, either.

China Southern Airlines Ltd.
SHA: 600029, A-shares; HKG: 0753, H-shares; NYSE: ZNH, ADR; OTC: CHKIF
Three-year trend: profits up 29.7 percent, revenues up 34.1 percent

China Southern is planning to use its base to become a major link to China's new trading partners in Africa. They fly Guangzhou to Lagos already and are instituting the first direct flight to Angola as part of ten new international routes announced at the start of 2007.

Hainan Airlines Co., Ltd.
SHA: 600221, A-shares; 900945, B-shares
Three-year trend: profits up 100.3 percent, revenues up 48 percent

Based on the resort island, Hainan is the fourth largest airline in China in terms of revenue. In 2006, it was awarded three top prizes for "safety, flight on-time rate, and customer satisfaction" by CAAC, which is significant for an industry plagued by delays. The airline is focusing on shorter hops with its new brand, Great New China Express; will consolidate its three regional subsidiaries; and has just purchased one hundred smaller planes from Embraer of Brazil (SAO [São Paulo exchange]: EMBR3, EMBR4; NYSE: ERJ, ADR).

Budget airlines are also testing their wings in China. Chungiu Ltd., a subsidiary of a travel agency of the same name, operates out of Shanghai to provide package tours. Juneyao Airlines, targeting frequent business travelers, expects to expand to thirteen aircraft in 2007. OK Air, supplementing passengers with air freight, has operated out of Tianjin since 2005. Look for their future listings.

Beijing Capital International Airport Co., Ltd.
HKG: 0694, H-shares; OTC: BJCHF
Three-year trend: profits up 43.7 percent, revenues up 0.84 percent

Would you like to have a direct stake in O'Hare, LAX, or the new Denver International? If you can't do it here, do it in China. With so many of China's newly expanded airports seeking the prestige of public listings, this has become a great way to cash in on the growth in Chinese aviation. And the Olympics are coming to this greatly modernized facility.

Xiamen International Airport Co., Ltd.
SHA: 600897, A-shares
Three-year trend: profits up 59.6 percent, revenues up 34.5 percent

Also deserving a look, Xiamen is the main destination for flights between China and the Philippines, as many Chinese Filipinos originally come from Fujian province (just across from Taiwan).

Shanghai International Airport Co., Ltd.
SHA: 600009, A-shares
Three-year trend: profits up 17.2 percent, revenues up 25.6 percent

Another world-class facility that will see more traffic. Built in the new area of Pudong in 1999, it can handle sixty million passengers a year, but will be expecting more during the Shanghai World's Fair 2010.

Watch out, Lonely Planet! Instead of using camel caravans, today's Marco Polos are buckling up. Like him, they will be bringing back word of wondrous sights in the East.

7

Agriculture: Have You Invested Yet?

S oybeans just aren't very sexy. Rice paddies are no field of dreams. Fruit orchards don't make for front-page headlines like Chinese yuppies driving Ferraris or boom towns that make all the world's hula hoops.

But what about the news that China, with one of the lowest percentages of arable land, already ranks number one in the world in farm output? Surely, there's plenty of thrills in unleashing the productivity of mankind's biggest single chunk of demographics: China's rural population, set officially in 2005 at 940 million.

Government initiatives, more efficient processing, and an astounding rise in specialized exports have started a big turnaround in the Chinese countryside. 2006 was a banner year: a 14.1 percent jump in China's farm production with a 20 percent increase in prices. Pushed by world markets and anti-protectionist WTO regulations that I'll outline below, the state has recently reduced ancient taxes while increasing incentives and investments to help nurture a long-delayed transformation of farming into modern agribusiness.

While strategies multiply as fast as appetites, a high-stakes race is on to establish the Middle Kingdom's versions of Archer Daniels

Midland, General Mills, and Kellogg. From feedlots to fine wines, this is where China may offer bushels of unrealized investment potential.

Like many other travelers, I was surprised at first to hear Chinese commonly greet one another by asking politely, "Have you eaten yet?" What follows are some of the opportunities to be found in China's new answers to that old question. With the Chinese leadership finally taking agriculture seriously, perhaps you should, too.

Growing Pains

China's present rulers have reason to be concerned about their vast farming community. For centuries, peasant uprisings helped topple even the most exalted emperors. Back in the 1980s, China's reform process was jump-started among this crucial group. Deng Xiaoping wisely chose the countryside to showcase market reforms by freeing farmers from producing for inefficient communes and abolished subsistence-level price controls. Under what was called the Household Responsibility System, the central government allowed farm families to engage in private enterprise with surplus yields, previously illegal in the Communist state. This incentive-based system worked, bringing in record harvests in 1982, 1983, and 1984 for grain, cotton, and other crops. Furthermore, it encouraged farmers to be entrepreneurs in other aspects of their lives. Private markets emerged, and rural towns became centers of commerce and trade. In the early years of reform, these rural businesses became the fastest-growing sector of China's economy, growing at a rate of 20 to 30 percent annually.

By 1987 over half the rural economy consisted of nonagricultural activities. Villages were prospering. I could see that for myself when I cruised around southeastern China in 1986. All over, the shacks where farmers used to live were being replaced with modern two-story houses—some fronted with statuary. Rising rural incomes and higher-quality foodstuffs combined to convince leaders to let urban

China off its socialized leash as well. Plus, the added tax revenues from villages and townships booming with new small industry helped fund infrastructure upgrades everywhere.

Since then, urban and rural have switched places. Once the country's manufacturing and service sectors took off, Chinese agriculture, tied to antiquated machinery and small plots (at last count, two hundred million small-scale households), just couldn't keep up. Accounting for 50.2 percent of China's GDP in 1952, agriculture has dropped to only 15 percent in 2005, generating less than 5 percent of the state till. The disparity between urban and rural incomes, with city people earning 2.6 times more in 1978, increased to 3.2 times in 2006. And in spite of the entrepreneurial wave sweeping the nation, China's countryside remained relatively unproductive, with one farmhand for every acre (compared with a single farmworker for every 140 acres in the United States). Even more telling, statistics say the "value added" worth of one rural Chinese worker is still two hundred times less than his or her American equivalent. No wonder men eighteen to forty are leaving the land to work in cities, so that larger "dragonhead" firms end up leasing abandoned tracts of land and bringing in more mechanized equipment.

With frequent protests over living standards and corruption, social unrest in China's countryside is a growing concern. Of even greater concern to China's economy is the low spending power of these 60 percent of the country's consumers. So the Chinese government focused its most recent Five-Year Plan heavily on closing the gap between city and country. Chinese politicians as high up as current premier, Wen Jiabao, have been out pressing the flesh at village weddings to talk up government promises of cleaner water, increased electrification, and a computerized generation of country schoolhouses. A record US$42 billion investment in agrarian infrastructure is backing up the talk. The government aims to boost funds for agricultural research and to establish more efficient irrigation systems, retail markets, and e-commerce. And such support, in turn, will help create plenty of opportunities for private investors.

Given their concern for the vast bulk of their population, Chinese negotiators for the WTO agreement won the right to continue to subsidize improvements and equipment for farmers up to a generous 8.5 percent of agricultural output. Along with help for farmers upgrading equipment have come measures to privatize bank cooperatives, leading to the doubling of farm loans between 2001 and 2005. Since taking effect in 2001, the WTO provisions have also allowed the Chinese government to continue paying farmers for some basic staples at prices above those of the international market—a tack they took after seeing acreage for planting rice, wheat, and corn shrink between 2001 and 2004.

But WTO provisions specified China's right to import products without going through state-trading enterprises or middlemen. This has helped curb the pricing and quota-setting power of state-financed monopolies in fields like tobacco and cotton—while allowing foreign firms more access to transport and distribution sectors. Chinese tariffs on imports of soybean oil, wine, and corn were lowered generally in half, from prohibitive levels to reasonable ones. This competition has forced Chinese farms to get more efficient in a hurry, which has meant breaking up the traditional small-plot system and has also caused the Chinese government to let go their loyalty to a costly "100 percent self-sufficiency" policy in feeding the country.

As a result, the total price tag for agricultural imports rose between 2002 and 2004 from around US$10 billion to US$25 billion. Such imports of largely United States–grown corn, wheat, and soybeans may look like a potential sign of China's weakness. On the contrary, these imports provide more indications of China's food boom—and offer more ways to get in on it, by looking at the U.S. and European firms best positioned to be longtime suppliers. Actually, the Chinese economy doesn't lose but gains from allowing the marketplace to dictate a more rational use of their precious soil. It makes perfect sense for land-scarce China to continue as an importer of land-intensive crops like wheat and cotton that they couldn't manage as well or afford, and for their farmers to concentrate on exporting. According to one World Bank estimate, China's overall economy could benefit by

US$5 billion if a reduction in basic grain growing continues through 2010.

China's tax men have likewise made a clean break from the traditional view that those on the land should support desk-bound officials. Since 2004, twenty of China's provinces have suspended all taxes on grain yields. In 2006, the central government even took the unprecedented step of removing a surcharge on each farm family, a surcharge that had been in place since 1958—and had existed in some form or other for 2,600 years! This was more than symbolic, since the household tax previously accounted for 3 percent of government revenue nationwide. One of China's new pollsters (another burgeoning industry) reported that relief from this ancient burden made "98 percent of farmers happy." I wonder who the other 2 percent were!

New agricultural firms that contribute to making basic foodstuffs healthier can also get tax write-offs. For instance, Bodisen Biotech, cited below, can claim exemption from agricultural and income taxes because it makes new, environmentally friendly fertilizers.

As modern agribusiness in the manner of developing countries is taking root, information about yields and prices is also becoming more reliable—of great significance to investors who need to base decisions on accurate information. During the Great Leap Forward, communal farms would hurriedly prop up old wheat stalks climbing to fantastical size to win favor when Chairman Mao's train steamed past. Until very recently, provincial leaders regularly overestimated harvests to make themselves look better, and state trading monopolies have been as secretive about food reserves as some nations are about uranium fuel rods. But China's burgeoning agricultural firms are getting the message that the entry fee for operating on the world market is proper auditing, testing, and labeling. There may be some tainted crops and bad publicity along the way—unfortunate for world consumers, though not so bad for investors, as the temporary problems might lead to investment opportunities—but China will learn in fits and starts to regulate its food industries more tightly, honestly, and openly.

With new profits made in local currency, investing in Chinese agriculture may also be a neat way of getting in on the inevitable upward evaluation of China's renminbi. There's just one catch. Because its process of reform has lagged behind, agriculture remains more volatile—open to sudden shifts caused by droughts or floods, world commodity prices or the vagaries of remaining trading monopolies. The quality and safety problems of some Chinese export foods, as in the summer of 2007, are an example. But there could be significant rewards for those companies that best soothe China's growing pains.

Jim's Sino Files: Goodbye Communes, Hello Combines

COFCO International Ltd.

HKG: 0506, H-shares (as China Foods Ltd.); OTC: CFITF
Three-year trend: profits up 257.9 percent, revenues up 54.9 percent

Looking for cooking oil, wine, chocolate, flour, animal feed? COFCO, headquartered in Hong Kong, is positioned to be the all-powerful provider, a major conglomerate with its fingers in much of the food industry. This outgrowth of a large state firm begun in 1952 has made a smooth transition, going public in 1999 and performing solidly. It's even one of the partner bottlers of Coca-Cola. If big makes you comfortable, COFCO is part of the Fortune 500, its overall trading having accounted for as much as 4 percent of China's imports and exports in cereals, oils, and foodstuffs. The company announced in 2007 that it plans to list its separate business units within five years.

Shanghai Dajiang (Group) Stock Co., Ltd.

SHA: 600695, A-shares; 900919, B-shares
Three-year trend: US$6.97 million loss up from US$30.8 million loss, revenues down 28.7 percent

Though shares prices have been down as it reorganizes, Dajiang seems determined to become one of China's big food brokers by expanding its core business of livestock feeds, mainly for pigs and poultry. They've gone into chicken parts in a big way, and are retailing everything from pork balls to frozen burgers and vow to "develop domestic local special flavor [*sic*] and exotic flavor of Europe, America, Southeast Asia and Latin America in order to meet requirement of different consumers."

China Animal Husbandry Industry Co., Ltd.
SHA: 600195, A-shares
Three-year trend: profits down 46.7 percent, revenues down 78.7 percent

Another major supplier of feeds, under its Hualo brand, as well as animal vaccines.

Haitong Food Group Co., Ltd.
SHA: 600537, A-shares
Three-year trend: profits up 41.4 percent, revenues up 6.4 percent

Headquartered in the fertile Yangtze River Delta, Haitong processes two hundred types of frozen, canned, and dehydrated products. It has been stressing "green foods" and claims rigorous testing procedures for pesticides. It also exports Japanese-style fare to the island and to South Korea, though it is adjusting to new Japanese standards set recently.

The Great Chinese Takeout

Over the centuries, China's Good Earth, as U.S. novelist Pearl Buck romanticized it, has hardly been good to its people. The inescapable fact is that China has only 7 percent of the world's cultivation area to feed over 20 percent of the world's population. To illustrate another way, China has three fourths the acreage of the United States, with which to feed four and a half times the number of mouths.

Traveling close to the land on my bike cruises, I passed practically every kind of discouraging patch of dirt: hardscrabble plots, rocky gorges, sheer desert. But thanks to a collective knack for horticulture with millennia-old roots, it was often a matter of inches before barren ground gave way to tidy rows laden with leafy greens (in fact, the Chinese invented the concept of laying seed in neat rows). Since being freed from their communes, Chinese farmers have engineered, through multiple harvests and fertilizers, a yield-per-acre rate that exceeds the world average in nearly every area, and far bests the United States when it comes to garden vegetables.

China's leaders have remained committed to seeing the country feed itself: a 1996 study by the State Council, "China's Grain Problem," made a commitment to the goal of 95 percent self-sufficiency. And remarkably, they've done it in most areas. In 2002, for instance, when the first year of WTO membership lowered tariffs and many predicted that imports of key grains like wheat would leap upward, China actually became a net exporter of foodstuffs for the first time. Despite its hungry consumers, the trend is continuing. Between 2000 and 2004, China jumped from ninth to fourth in the world as an agricultural exporter by emphasizing products in which it had a comparative advantage.

When I visited the desert oasis town of Hami on my travels, I learned how the emperor in Beijing could get to sample one of his favorite freshly picked Hami melons within a few days. To further speed and streamline deliveries, China is in the process of setting up an international trade center for fruits and vegetables in Chengdu, capital of the "breadbasket" province of Sichuan. With China's farmers no longer restricted to toting their goods on bicycles, the value of their exports doubled in just under a decade—and since WTO membership in 2001, the push has gathered further momentum, not merely in terms of higher yields but also in modern shipping, juice facilities, frozen foods, and new emphasis on labor-intensive crops that China can produce at great competitive advantage.

Fruit orchards, for instance, need to be pruned and protected constantly. The Shandong town of Feicheng, which has produced peaches beloved by the emperors for centuries, won recent entry in the *Guinness World Records* for the world's largest single peach orchard— yielding three million half-pound peaches in one harvest. And 2005 saw further record growth from growers: the US$189 million worth of fruit exports was a 66 percent jump from the previous year. And the cost of producing such fruit in China is 40 percent of what it is in the United States, and 20 percent of what it is in Japan.

No wonder most of the Fuji apples are from Chinese trees! Or that apple juice exports are exploding: from 1994 to 2000, the value of Chinese juice sales went up eighteenfold. And that's without much help from the Chinese themselves, whose per capita juice consumption is less than two liters per year, compared with an average of forty liters in developed countries. While we all know that nothing is as "all-American as apple pie," an amazing 95 percent of concentrate used in American apple juices comes from China. While Chinese juice makers were fined for dumping their product at less than half of prevailing world prices, that hasn't stopped them from making further inroads into the economies of American apple-growing regions.

There's lots to savor in this version of Chinese takeout, even if it's done in ship holds instead of cardboard cartons. Russia is also a key market for items like coconuts, grapes, pears, and dried apricots. Chinese mushrooms and garlic are also making their way into supermarkets throughout the world. Mandarin oranges, closer to our tangerines and symbols of rebirth like our Christmas trees, flood the rest of Asia during the Lunar New Year. But boxes of all sorts of Chinese citrus are becoming commonplace throughout all seasons.

Now the Chinese have been eyeing the European Union's citrus-hungry market and making enough strides there that Spanish growers, like American ones, have been squawking for more protection. Chinese strawberries, too, are making inroads. Major Belgian jam maker Materne-Confilux made a recent splash by admitting they'd chosen Chinese berries produced by up-and-coming Baoding Binghua Food at half the price of Polish ones. They just can't beat China's prices.

Jim's Sino Files: More Than Juicy Fruit

SDIC Zhonglu Fruit Juice Co., Ltd.
SHA: 600962, A-shares
Three-year trend: profits up 60.9 percent, revenues up 54.9 percent

Zhonglu produces apple, pear, carrot, and date—yes, date—juices. It accounts for 10 percent of world market share, providing ingredients for conglomerates like Nestlé. In 2004, Zhonglu became the first semipublic Chinese company in the concentrated juice processing industry to be listed.

Yantai North Andre Juice Co., Ltd.
HKG: 8259, H-shares
Three-year trend: profits down 23.4 percent, revenues up 39.5 percent

A newcomer of just a decade, this firm has made huge investments in modern processing facilities, as well as research and development of such pressing matters as "secondary sedimentation removal technology" to become a leader in the burgeoning apple bonanza. So far, 95 percent of the business is for export. The Shandong company's concentrated Clear Juice won a top China brands award, and its plants, which also make jam pectin, are even kosher.

China Huiyuan Juice Group Ltd.
HKG: 1886, H-shares
Three-year trend: profits up 851.1 percent, revenues up 78.3 percent

Huiyuan raised US$307 million with its March 2007 IPO. It is number one in domestic sales and exports as well. Groupe Danone, Warburg Pincus, and Uni-President are among the strategic investors.

Oriental Food (Holdings) Ltd.
SIN: 5FI, S-shares
Three-year trend: profits down 83.1 percent, revenues up 0.01 percent

Despite this company's middling performance, peanuts deserve a mention. They are one of China's oldest crops, and not a banquet in China begins without them. This peanut firm exports to Japan and Korea and makes oil, powders, and other by-products of the snack.

Feeding the Demand

The first time I went to China, most of the banquets in my honor seemed an excuse for local hosts to gobble scarce delicacies (like a bit of beef or, if lucky, a whole fish). Now every respectable restaurant has full fish tanks, and meat processors are seeing 30 percent jumps in sales each year. At last count, 312 companies helped with what amounts to 71 percent of all the meat production in Asia.

China is already number one in the world in pork production, second in chicken, and third in beef. When it comes to livestock in general, quantities of beef and chicken raised in China quadrupled from 1990 to 1998 (while milk went up six times, eggs eight times). Most of this is meant for domestic consumption—especially as urbanites seek more quality items on their tables and the food service industry continues to expand rapidly.

That means everything in the agricultural cycle, like feedlots—even tractor and farm equipment manufacturers—are benefiting from increased demand. They don't call it the "food chain" for nothing. For example, the feed needed to raise China's animals went from 0.6 million tons in 1978 to 63 million twenty years later. So domestic feed manufacturers increased output at a rate of 15 percent a year through the nineties. In a recent five-year period, the number of mills producing feed went up ten times.

In turn, that's led to a far greater need for corn, soybeans, and other products that go into high-protein feeds. It's the appetites of these animals, more than humans, that has pushed up China's purchase of grains and other proteins. Amazingly, thanks to United States–style herds, the land that invented soy sauce has become the largest purchaser of soybeans on earth. They purchased US$3 billion from American farmers, 40 percent of world sales in 2005. Already, the Dalian Commodity Exchange—one of three futures exchanges in China, along with those in Shanghai and Zhengzhou—trades more soybean contracts than they do in Chicago. So looking at American soy exporters is an indirect way to invest in China as well.

As buyer or seller, China will be a major force in agriculture and commodities markets from now on. But four fifths of all China's meat still comes from small producers, which means companies that can help with tracking, labeling, consolidating, and adding hygiene to China's meat pipeline should also be in demand. As plot sizes increase, there will also be fewer old-fashioned one-cylinder tractors like those that used to block my path on many rural roads, looking like the illegitimate offspring of rickshaws and lawn mowers. These are being replaced by bigger, more advanced machinery, as U.S. and even Indian firms eye a growing Chinese demand aided by government payouts to farmers of up to a third of the cost. But sturdy Chinese machinery brands are also increasingly exported throughout the world, and gaining cache at very competitive prices. Already, there's a Chinese Tractor Owners Association based in the good old U.S. of A.

Jim's Sino Files: Seed Money

Henan Shuanghui Investment and Development Co.
SHE: 000895, A-shares
Three-year trend: profits up 49.3 percent, revenues up 50.5 percent

Foreign investors appear to be salivating over China's meat processing industry. Counting on a steady rise in meat consumption, trader Goldman Sachs and CDH Investment have just completed a joint-venture near-US$250-million investment in this state-held processor, claimed to be China's largest.

China Yurun Food Group Ltd.
HKG: 1068, H-shares
Three-year trend: profits up 188.7 percent, revenues up 82.7 percent

Another processor attracting foreign investors, this one focused largely on pig slaughtering and frozen pork sales. Besides, they are one Chinese firm that knows how to make maple-cured bacon and pepperoni.

Gansu Dunhuang Seed Co., Ltd.
SHA: 600354, A-shares
Three-year trend: profits down 57 percent, revenues up 19.8 percent

Astoundingly, China devotes more acreage to corn than any other country except the United States, and half of that is in remote Gansu province. Now DuPont has just entered into a joint venture with Gansu Dunhuang to produce more hybrid corn seed. The Chinese company also aids in cultivation of cotton and melons across China.

Shandong Denghai Seeds Co., Ltd.
SHE: 002041, A-shares
Three-year trend: profits down 92.9 percent, revenues down 4.7 percent

U.S. group Pioneer has bought nearly half the shares of Shandong Denghai, founded in 2000 and specializing in corn as well as vegetables, with an enormous production capacity (for example, twenty-five million pounds of maize seed per annum). Started from a research industry in 1985 with an investment of US$2,400, they now report US$116.1 million in assets. Founder Li Denghai is known as "the king of Maize" for having topped the world record in corn yield per hectare by over sixteen tons.

Jiangsu Yueda Yancheng Tractor Manufacture Co., Ltd.
SHA: 600805, A-shares
Three-year trend: profits up 19.8, revenues up 44.4 percent

The bigger the supermarket carts, the bigger the tractors. And Chinese tractors are becoming big business. Jiangsu Yueda is the manufacturer of the popular Jinma tractors and many more, including a Huanghai brand "Walking Tractor." Established in 1959, the company has the capacity to produce 110,000 machines annually, selling them in the United States, France, and the Middle East. And this holding company even manages a few major highways.

First Tractor Co., Ltd.
HKG: 0038, H-shares
Three-year trend: profits up 632.4 percent, revenues up 43.7 percent

First Tractor is another major player in agricultural machinery. But Hubei Machinery and Equipment Import & Export Corp., one of China's two hundred largest companies by turnover, is unlisted as yet.

From the Chairman to the Colonel

The Chinese are famous for eating just about anything. I know all too well from my close encounter with the famed purveyors of snake who slice out the gall bladder and squeeze the bile into a wine cocktail. But these days, China's adventurous eaters have gone beyond camel's paw to some truly exotic fare. What could be more bizarre in old Beijing than Philly cheesesteaks or pineapple-topped Hawaiian pizza? An influx of Western marketing and Western food is transforming an age-old diet based on vegetables and rice. That means big gains for newly enlarged sectors of agriculture.

In 1966, when Mao exhorted the Red Guards to "serve the people," they might have considered going into catering: starch accounted for 67 percent of calorie intake in China, with meat less than 4 percent, sweets 1.3 percent, and vegetables almost as scarce (around thirty pounds a year per person). Now rice is down from 37 percent to 27 percent, and meat and fish are four times as plentiful. With statues of Colonel Sanders outnumbering those of Mao, and the majority of new McDonald's found in China, there's even been a 40 percent rise in Chinese potato production to satisfy increasing demand for french fries. As Starbucks and Pizza Hut go gangbusters, too, that means a bigger slice of the market for cheese and milk—in a land where it is believed that a majority of the populace lacks the proper enzymes for digesting lactose.

As of 2006, China slurped up 13 percent of the world's milk supply. Given China's population, even modest percentage increases translate into substantial growth in dairy demand—and the demands have been increasing nearly 25 percent a year over the past decade. And given the experience of other Asian countries, there's plenty of room for growth. According to United States Department of Agriculture (USDA) statistics, South Korea consumes seven times more milk than China per capita, Taiwan eleven times, and Japan sixteen times.

No wonder that by 2002 there were already sixteen hundred enterprises involved in the China dairy industry. Some have even begun producing small amounts of sheep and buffalo cheese to take advantage of excess resources. Yogurt sales, especially with trendy new "probiotic" cultures, are rising at a similar level. In northern Liaoning province, dairy herds have tripled since 2000.

In every country I've visited, an economic surge is followed by the urge for high-calorie treats. With young people getting used to soda instead of tea, and more people able to afford ice cream and pastries, that means a big jump in demand for another of those basic world commodities. In fact, China has now jumped all the way to number five in terms of countries with a sweet tooth.

This has meant an annual shortfall of close to two million tons of sugar in recent years—even though China's sugar production increased thirty-four-fold during the eighties and nineties and now ranks number four in the world. Yet the industry remains in flux. Competition from imports since the 2001 WTO agreement have lowered prices by around 30 percent. This means that in 2006, around 150 smaller sugar growers were facing bankruptcy. Other factors were poor weather and, yes, the Chinese consumer's turn to less fattening artificial sweeteners.

Jim's Sino Files: Fast-Food Rations

Nanning Sugar Manufacturing Co., Ltd.
SHE: 000911, A-shares
Three-year trend: profits up 32.1 percent, revenues up 56.7 percent

Responsible for 4 percent of China's total sugar production and export to Europe, the Middle East, and the rest of Asia, while supplying steady clients like Pepsi and Coke.

China Sun Bio-Chem Tech Group Co., Ltd.
SIN: C86, S-shares; OTC: CBTKF
Three-year trend: profits up 63.8 percent, revenues up 109.7 percent

Addressing the growing popularity of alternatives to sugar, Sun Bio-Chem plans to produce sweeteners made from corn. They already have a big capacity for producing cornstarch, the essential thickener in Chinese cuisine, plus products like gluten, liquor, and even, yes, ethanol for automotive needs—with a one-hundred-thousand-ton capacity plant in Shenyang, a major city in China's northeast.

China Mengniu Dairy Co., Ltd.
HKG: 2319, H-shares; OTC: CIADF
Three-year trend: profits up 120.1 percent, revenues up 125.2 percent

Mengniu is a top seller of milk in China and Hong Kong. The company produces milk powder, liquid milk, yogurt, ice cream, and assorted milk-based beverages. The name of the company and the brand literally translates into "Mongolian cow," but it is also a homonym for "strong cow." Mengniu's cleverest marketing scheme was sponsoring what turned into the Chinese equivalent of *American Idol*—appetizingly named *Mengniu Yogurt Super Girl Contest*. The show's final episode drew four hundred million viewers in 2005, one of the most-watched TV shows in mainland China in history. The company even turned its search for a new CEO into a publicity stunt—placing ads in *Business Week*—but ended up appointing the mastermind of *Super Girl*.

American Dairy, Inc.
NYSE: ADY, ADR

Three-year trend: profits up 218 percent, revenues up 228.1 percent

This dairy is hardly American at all, but a holding company for Heilongjiang province's Feihe Dairy Company and three-plus wholly owned subsidiaries. They produce a variety of milk products and powders, even walnut powders. The 2006 third-quarter report indicated increases in revenues of 129 percent and 157 percent, respectively, in gross profits from the previous two years.

Angel Yeast Co., Ltd.
SHA: 600298, A-shares

Three-year trend: profits up 42.5 percent, revenues up 58.6 percent

Given the increase in Western-style baking and its many by-products, this youngest of the world's top five yeast makers may be well positioned. Its by-products are used in beer brewing, animal feeds, vitamins, and seasonings. They are helping cakes, and profits, rise in over sixty countries, including Africa.

Henan Lianhua Gourmet Powder Co., Ltd.
SHA: 600186, A-listed

Three-year trend: profits up 363.8 percent, revenues up 94.9 percent

But what's Chinese food without a dash of MSG? This is one of China's main manufacturers of the seaweed-based flavor enhancer favored by home and restaurant chefs (still marketed largely by its inventor, Japan's Ajinomoto, TYO: 2802). They also produce other essentials like cornstarch and are dabbling in "thermal and electric power."

New Kinds of Reds

When it comes to alcohol, Chinese are also turning to new ways of saying "Bottoms up!" Did you know that China is already the sixth-largest wine-producing country in the world? That over five hundred wineries have been established in a variety of Chinese climates, some by top European winemakers? Or that the secret ingredient in the world's finest dessert port is fortification with brandy made from Chinese vineyards?

At any Chinese banquet, you find groups of men besting one another in emptying glasses, then bottles, of beer. And Tsingtao remains one of China's most recognized brands, the only Chinese entry in the top fifty on Forbes's list of the world's best four hundred companies. One of my favorite places in China, the large port city of Qingdao (sometimes spelled "Tsingtao") in Shandong province, was a German enclave, and its many church steeples look to be straight out of Bavaria. So are the brewing techniques first passed down there.

Yet another of Shandong's famous spots is Yantai's Chateau Changyu, a quaint European-style attraction run by the Yantai Changyu winery—China's largest—where visitors can pick grapes, indulge in wine tasting, and, for under a buck, tour a museum of Chinese wine history. The ultimate expression of China's new appetites has to be the country's purple passion for Western-style wine—made with grapes, that is, to the tune of US$2.2 billion in annual 2005 earnings.

If you hear talk about "reds" in China these days, it's most likely referring to corked bottles of a native vintage. Estimates say the number of Chinese wine drinkers is increasing 15 percent annually. There's room for growth in a hard-drinking society where wine lags behind all other alcoholic beverages, with consumption per head still only 6 percent of the world average. As a result, a handful of China's homegrown vintners have a shot at becoming the Gallos and Mondavis of the Asia-Pacific. Which sometimes means the Chinese get carried away: the port city of Dalian has actually formed something called the Maritime Biological Brewery to try to make wine out of fish!

So far, China's connoisseurs tend to like their bubbly a tad sweet: the common practice is to spike wine with 7-UP! You might do the same with bottles priced to sell at US$1.65. Today, there's a whole class of experts trying to find the best merlot to match with sea cucumber. Take a table in Chinese dining spots these days and packs of pretty young handmaidens descend upon you—pitching wine brands emblazoned on skintight dresses, hoping you'll uncork their employer's chosen Cathay chardonnay.

Several local labels are already gaining respect from the fussy French. Camus, best known for cognac, will feature Dragon Seal—founded in 1910 and already exporting to twenty countries—at duty-free shops the company runs in airports worldwide. Yet as China's drinkers grow more discerning, there's always the risk that foreign imports will end up dominating the field (making import firms a better bet). With tariffs on imported wines lowered nearly 100 percent over three years as part of the 2001 WTO agreement, China has already replaced Japan as the biggest market for French vintages—with a 60 percent increase in imported spirits over the same period. It's only a matter of time before Shanghai sophisticates will be celebrating, as they do in Tokyo, the annual jet shipment of Beaujolais Nouveau.

But experienced vintners like Spain's Torres are putting their roots down in China. And the big Chinese players aren't just watching their vineyards grow. In 2005, Yantai Changyu gained publicity (but no known takers) by offering a hefty US$175,000 salary for an experienced wine master—"preferably from Bordeaux," the ad said—willing to relocate to the rocky hillsides of northern China. I'll bet plenty of Moutons and Rothschilds are ready to help the Chinese with their pressing task.

Jim's Sino Files: Spirits of the People

Yantai Changyu Pioneer Wine Co., Ltd.
SHE: 000869, A-shares; 200869, B-shares
Three-year trend: profits up 118.1 percent, revenues up 71 percent

Yantai Changyu has been around since 1892, before modern China itself came into being. In 1997, Yantai Changyu became the first Chinese winery ever listed on a mainland exchange. In 2005, Italian liqueur giant Saronno purchased 30 percent of the company. A major purchaser of bulk-imported wine to supplement its production, the company offers homegrown cabernets and a distinctly Chinese line known as Healthy Liquor, combining alcohol with herbal medicine. With over one hundred separate products, Yantai Changyu is China's largest winemaker, sharing just over half the market with its big-three competitors: Great Wall, Weilong, and Dynasty.

Dynasty Fine Wines Group Ltd.
HKG: 0828, H-shares
Three-year trend: profits down 31.7 percent, revenues up 38.5 percent

Managed from Hong Kong, this slickly run group puts out a vast variety of wines, including sparkling and brandy. Its better grapes are reserved for export and it relies on the expertise of Remy Cointreau, the French liqueur group that is Dynasty's second-largest shareholder.

Zhejiang GuYueLongShan Shaoxing Wine Co.
SHA: 600059, A-shares
Three-year trend: profits down 37 percent, revenues up 30 percent

Just because they've acquired a taste for the bubbly, that doesn't mean the Chinese are abandoning their traditional rice wines, favored for special occasions as well as cooking. And the historic city of Shaoxing, south of Shanghai, has been the mecca for Chinese-style wine-making over the centuries. In fact, the whole place reeks of the fermented output of numerous large competitors who guard their industrial secrets zealously and who also produce distinctive pottery bottles and jars.

Wuliangye Yibin Co., Ltd.
SHE: 000858, A-shares
Three-year trend: profits up 41.3 percent, revenues up 17.3 percent

Based in Sichuan, Wuliangye is another renowned distiller of various famed grain-based firewaters. It has also been extending its international reach and averaging 10-plus percent share returns.

Tsingtao Brewery Co., Ltd.
SHA: 600600, A-shares; HKG: 0168, H-shares; OTC: TSGTY, TSGTF
Three-year trend: profits up 41.3 percent, revenues up 17.3 percent

Everybody in the world, everyone who has ever been inside a Chinese restaurant anyhow, has heard of Tsingtao Brewery. You'll find its A-shares listed on the Shanghai exchange, with more shares listed on the Hong Kong exchange and traded on pink sheets in the United States. And Tsingtao accounts for 14 percent of the huge Chinese beer market—having gotten a big head start when founded by Germans in 1903. Today, it's not the Chinese government but U.S. giant Anheuser-Busch, also founded by German immigrants, that owns a 30 percent stake in Tsingtao and may be aiming for a controlling interest.

Beijing Yanjing Brewery Co., Ltd.
SHE: 000729, A-shares
Three-year trend: profits up 13.5 percent, revenues up 31.1 percent

One of many regional entries in the great race to share national billing with Tsingtao, Beijing Yanjing has been a solid performer from its base in China's capital, adding bottled waters, juices, teas, colas, and vinegars to its mix.

A Jolly Green Giant?

The first time I spied Chinese growing methods, they were about as organic as anything could get. I didn't realize at first, but those huts set in the midst of most fields weren't Oriental scarecrows or shrines. They were outhouses, conveniently located for easy distribution of human wastes gathered in "honey buckets" balanced at the end of wooden poles and distributed freely as cheap fertilizer.

Since then, the Chinese have loaded their fields with more chemicals than just about anywhere else on earth. (On average, Chinese farmers had been using double the amount of fertilizers used in the United States, some toxic enough to be banned here.) Given many past famines, it makes sense that peasants were focused on greater yields at any cost. No country has been quicker to adopt uncritically the benefits of "progress," including genetically modified seeds.

But all that is changing as quickly as you can say "Johnny Appleseed." World scrutiny, combined with China's need to market its products as safe and reliable, is driving Chinese agriculture to clean up its act. For example, stricter 2006 standards regulating chemical residues in Japan—already scandalized by frozen Chinese spinach that didn't pass muster—will affect some six thousand Chinese firms. Already, China has 11 percent of the organic growing land in the world; most likely, any organic pumpkin or sunflower seeds, kidney and black beans, will be from China. In fact, the country launched its own Organic Food Development Center as far back as 1994. Starting from virtually zero, China had, by 2003, zoomed past US$4 billion in sales of organic produce from eight hundred certified organic companies.

And unlike in the West, where organic farming was started by small, independent rebels, China's chemical-free industry—driven by low wages and high prices that help create profit margins of up to 70 percent gross—is carving out big tracts of the country's pristine northeast. Where it once was viewed as a world polluter, China's competitive advantage is turning it into the world's next green giant.

But agriculture is merely moving in tandem with the rest of a society that has reached the stage where mere subsistence gives way to concerns for a better quality of life. Pick up the state-run newspapers in China these days and the headlines are all about initiatives related to Beijing's pledge to stage a green Olympics. China has even got its own green trains that feature environmental lectures as they pass through the mountains of Kunming and the grasslands of Mongolia. Amtrak, take note.

Chinese provinces had associations for promoting healthier diet alternatives before "organic" ever got translated into Chinese—setting up pilot green food development areas and serving an industry with 2,836 firms. Believe it or not, the latest batch of Chinese astronauts even made it a point to tell the world they were surviving in space on a diet of chemical-free green food produced under special conditions at China's "Aerospace Town." These astronauts ate plenty of rice, along with dehydrated cuttlefish balls and fruits like—yes—the emperor's favorite, Hami melon! Tell that to the American spacemen who once pitched Tang, that sweet powdered drink!

After all, the Chinese were the first to espouse the view that "you are what you eat," seeing food's balance of yin and yang effects in the body as closely allied with medicine. So it makes sense that China's growing middle class has begun to join the worldwide demand for cleaner and healthier food. Organic items are appearing in markets throughout urban China now—Shanghai even has its own all-organic "O" market. Not only can you find plenty of organic Chinese teas (Jiangxi province's Wuyuan Organic Foods, as yet unlisted, sold US$3 million worth last year) but also organic lychees and—say it ain't so—organic pig face.

Such domestic demand can only increase—causing large Japanese concerns like Asahi Breweries to invest in organic produce aimed at China's own internal market. Ironically enough, much of the land being set aside to feed health-conscious Westerners is in Heilongjiang and Jilin, areas where so-called educated youth once were sent to starve by "learning from the peasants" in forced labor camps. But it's China's basic competitive advantage, enabling them to grow labor-intensive and small-scale specialty organic crops far more cheaply than anywhere else, that will drive this growing industry.

Jim's Sino Files: Greener Pastures

Chaoda Modern Agriculture (Holdings) Ltd.
HKG: 0682, H-shares
Three-year trend: profits up 34.8 percent, revenues up 50.3 percent

This pioneering company has persevered through droughts, floods, and the 2003 SARS outbreak to produce 150 species of organic vegetables and fruits: edible fungi, organic teas, exotic fruits, as well as organic livestock. More remarkable, only 30 percent of its sales are overseas.

Pine Agritech Ltd.
SIN: P39, S-shares
Three-year trend: profits up 293 percent, revenues up 198.9 percent

Pine Agritech manufactures U.S. soy imports into low-fat processed soybean-based products, including everything from soy protein isolates and cooking oil to a healthy syrup.

Bodisen Biotech, Inc.
AMEX: BBC; AIM (London Alternative Investment Market): BODI; OTC: BBCZ
Three-year trend: profits up 180.3 percent, revenues up 168.6 percent

Think Chinese farmers will take a chance on organic fertilizers? Then take a chance on Bodisen Biotech. This Maryland-based company, with production lines in Yangling, is trying to rebound from a 2006 scandal regarding full disclosure of its assets. But Forbes previously named the innovative Bodisen the sixteenth-fastest-growing company in China, thanks to its certified organic biopesticides and biofertilizers. Can Bodisen undo the damage as China's growers undo theirs?

China BlueChemical Ltd.
HKG: 3983, H-shares
Three-year trend: profits up 118.1 percent, revenues up 71 percent

In case you want to cover all bases, chemical companies should continue to benefit from agricultural expansion. Sinopec, cited earlier, is the number one Chinese producer of nitrogenous fertilizers and urea. China Blue, the fertilizer unit of CNOOC, staged an IPO in September 2006.

In place of the Cultural Revolution, China is staging an organic revolution. I guess what goes around, comes around. Even human fertilizer.

8

Health, Education, Housing:
Serve the Masses

W hen I first went to China, nearly everybody was tied to the apron strings of the Communist Party. Foreign journalists were shocked when they had to register their pet dogs and cats as members of their company's "work unit." Rudimentary health care, education, housing, and pensions, plus factory meals—in a system where there really was a free lunch, if cold rice was your cup of tea— were offered at a pittance as part of a "safety net" that probably felt more like a straitjacket. Insurance, an unknown Western concept, came from faith in the care of "Great Helmsman" Mao, who offered communal state farms and not State Farm dividends.

But ever since the reforms of the late 1980s, that iron rice bowl began splitting into cracks, then finally busted into smithereens. "Womb to tomb" has been replaced by "pay as you go." Now it's every Chinese for himself or herself, with next to nothing guaranteed but everything possible. Pensions are especially under threat, with fewer children supporting more elders (most of whom worked for almost nothing in their prime). This has meant improvements for some, hardships for others, and tremendous competition among the bold enterprises that have leaped to fill the void in China's social contract.

At stake is nothing less than the welfare of a nation and a billion monthly dividend checks in the mail. As the country gropes toward a workable health care system, specialized choices in education, and housing that isn't just for developers, investors can profit from the ways China's privatized system is approaching the public good.

A Healthy Prognosis

In the West, Chinese medicine conjures images of acupuncture needles and dried deer antler powder. In fact, China has produced brilliant doctors since the days when they carved their prescriptions on tortoiseshells. But the creation of a modern health care system has barely begun, and may be one of those key battlegrounds between private and public interests—with a prognosis for vast expenditures and expansion.

After the founding of the People's Republic in 1949, itinerant semi-trained "barefoot doctors" extended health care to many areas that had never known it before. In just over three decades, life expectancy rose from thirty-five to seventy, and infant mortality decreased from two hundred to thirty-one per one thousand. In the early 1980s, when economic reforms were beginning, 71 percent of China's populace still had access to state-run health services, at virtually no cost. By just over a decade later, this figure had dropped to 21 percent.

Obviously that isn't good news. According to the World Health Organization, China's health care system before 1980 performed better than in other countries of comparable development; since 1980, it has ranked lower than most. Five years back, the WHO ranked Chinese medical care delivery at a lowly 144th in the world—below even most African countries. As far back as the 1960s, China had virtually eliminated such ancient scourges as smallpox, cholera, and tuberculosis. Now such diseases are making a comeback. There were almost 1.4 million tuberculosis cases in China in 2004, making it the leading infectious cause of death.

Adding further worry is a generally aging populace and the 30 percent annual increase in HIV/AIDS from the 840,000 known cases in 2004. After years of denial, the Chinese government broadcast President Hu Jintao shaking hands with an AIDS victim and has set a goal of containing HIV infections to fewer than 1.5 million by 2010. Funding to fight the disease was doubled between 2004 and 2005. The frightening 2003 outbreak of the SARS virus also cost China an estimated US$36.3 billion in economic impact. Afterward, the Chinese government committed funding to improving disease control centers.

Health care costs, to individuals and society, are rising even faster. In 1978, the percentage of health care costs paid by the individual was practically zero. The share of total health care expenditure paid by individuals had risen to 53.6 percent in 2004. The full bill for medical services rose from US$1.7 billion in 1980 to US$92 billion in 2004. Again, the rural vs. urban split is key: most benefits go to wealthier urbanites, who can pay for better care and even pay for scandalous yet common under-the-table bribes required to get attentive nursing or examinations.

While urbanites can get the best that money can buy, a 2003 government survey found that 60 percent of rural residents cannot afford hospitals altogether, with 90 percent uninsured and unseen by doctors. But even a recent plan that gives peasants access to doctors for a dollar per year was considered too costly for many. While nearly four hundred million Chinese have some health coverage through employee plans, this does nothing to help cover the country's immense migrant labor force. No wonder Chinese leaders talk of improving the health service system as the linchpin of any plan to improve the lot of the Chinese countryside.

As of 2004, China spent only 4.7 percent of GDP on health care, compared with 8 percent or more in developed countries (and 16 percent in the United States). In early 2007, as part of making health care a major priority, Premier Wen Jiabao announced the creation of a trial "co-operative medical service" throughout "80 percent of China" by 2010. The state will double subsidies to US$1.53 billion and offer small amounts to pay medical bills for all rural dwellers. This is a first step toward meeting the huge increased demands of a population that isn't just currently underserved but that by 2020 will have 170 million people over sixty, in addition to the number with chronic illnesses. Old age pensions and other forms of social security will be bolstered by an added US$35.7 billion in 2007. At the same time, a finance vice minister announced that China will be actively encouraging more private investment in the health care industry, offering preferential tax policies to those who would help improve a nationwide system full of inefficiency and soaring costs. All this should mean benefits for emerging health care providers and those who invest in them.

In one 2003 study, only 8 percent of China's 12,599 hospitals, handling 3 percent of patients, was said to be run for profit. Out of twenty-nine thousand registered medical facilities, only sixty had foreign investors. Overseas investments in China's health services are rising, but in 2003, it was estimated at US$2 billion. Fully foreign-owned facilities are still not allowed. However, the idea of privatized hospitals is gaining currency. The ancient canal city of Suzhou, for one, just took private bids on its hospitals, and several in the area have been sold to foreign interests already.

At the same time, new regulations to hold down costs will impact spending by Chinese hospitals and consumers, in turn affecting foreign and domestic drug manufacturers. The amount public hospitals can charge for prescription drugs will be capped at 15 percent above the purchase price for the public hospitals, and medical devices and pacemakers will also be controlled. This will have a huge impact on drug sales: UNICEF states that 60 percent of China's health care spending goes to drugs, compared with the worldwide average of 15 percent—with hospitals in coastal cities making half their revenues from markups on medicine.

Western drugs, once used as a last resort, are now more commonly used. Pharmaceuticals in general are expanding, up a whopping 20 percent to sales of US$11.7 billion in 2005, with 75 percent Western drugs, 25 percent traditional Chinese. But the industry suffers a greater degree of regulation, so investors should approach this sector with some caution. Ongoing price caps could reduce margins from 30 percent to 15 percent. Compared to similar Western companies, Chinese drug manufacturers still spend only a fraction of their profits on R&D.

In fact, one estimate says 99 percent of Chinese Western-style medicines are copied from foreign models. With stricter enforcement of quality checks, a divestment of state-run companies, and a blacklisting of patent-breakers, there will be big shakedowns in this area. Safety problems—and scandals over tainted toothpaste—will occur. Unfortunate as these are, they may lead to buying opportunities. The industry is relatively small and low-tech in comparison with others, but local manufacturers have the advantage of owning their own dispensing pharmacies and maintaining close connections with hospitals. Also, dietary supplements are one area on the increase; the Chinese are discovering vitamins.

In an effort to obtain approval to sell their products abroad, Chinese drug makers are beginning to buy shares of companies overseas. Or they are channeling products through India, which, as a British commonwealth member, retains special advantages in registering drugs in the United Kingdom. From there, it's a small step to the rest of Europe. Yet many foreign firms are still reluctant to release the latest products in China due to theft of intellectual property. The government is trying to address this as well, and has cracked down on corruption with a wave of arrests across the country in 2007 aimed at stopping the fraudulent issuance of GMP (Good Marketing Procedure) certificates needed for drug manufacturing. While this news may be alarming about general drug safety, it can only be a good sign when state-run media publicize such a crackdown.

Where many facilities were once basic, the demand for medical equipment is now growing at a double-digit pace. The Chinese medical equipment market was estimated as being worth US$2.6 billion in 2005, and is slated to replace Japan's as the world's second-largest as clinics with little more than ginseng pills stock up on everything from CAT scan machines to heart monitors. For now, foreign brand names dominate the field, or are forging joint ventures with local companies as potential entry strategies into the Chinese market. Increasingly, larger international companies are also setting up research and development facilities in China. At this point, local manufacturers are involved in an intense competition at the low end. But they probably won't stay there for too long.

In recent months, there's even been talk of creating American-style HMO's—a once taboo term that is just entering the Chinese vocabulary. But a lot of red Chinese tape will still have to be cleared away before there is meaningful corporate involvement in upgrading patient care. It took five years of applications before the foreign-run Beijing United Family Hospital finally opened its doors. As the parent company reported, their Shanghai branch required 150 "chops" (official seals) before getting the green light to operate.

Jim's Sino Files: Prescriptions for Profit

China Medical Technologies, Inc.
NASDAQ: CMED, ADR
Three-year trend: profits up 223.3 percent, revenues up 235.7 percent

CMED markets cutting-edge ultrasound devices and has consistently been among the top performers of Chinese stocks listed in the United States—with a 2006 net profit margin rise of 53.53 percent. They've been acquiring specialized device manufacturers.

Sunray Holdings Limited
SIN: S38, S-shares
Three-year trend: profits up 24.7 percent, revenues up 28 percent

Sunray is a Singapore-based investment holding company that sells through subsidiaries a wide range of monitors and apparatus related to childbirth and cancer diagnosis. It lists only 154 employees yet seems to be steadily gaining value.

Harbin Pharmaceutical Group Co., Ltd.
SHA: 600664, A-shares
Three-year trend: profits up 75.5 percent, revenues up 28.2 percent

Harbin is becoming more competitive with a US$250 million capital infusion from two foreign investors, Warburg Pincus of New York and CITIC Capital of Hong Kong. That money will allow Harbin

Pharmaceutical to expand its R&D efforts—the company spends about 5 percent of revenue on R&D, exceptional for a Chinese drug maker yet just a third of what most multinationals spend. It is pursuing a Hong Kong listing.

Sinovac Biotech Ltd.
AMEX: SVA, ADR
Three-year trend: US$700,000 loss up from US$4.23 million loss, revenues up 138.1 percent

Sinovac has been way down for several years now compared with other Chinese stocks. But it has released the first combined hepatitis A&B vaccine developed by Chinese scientists, and the only competing vaccine has been unavailable in China. Sinovac has also been developing a SARS vaccine.

Tong Ren Tang Technologies Co., Ltd.
HKG: 8069, H-shares
Three-year trend: profits up 3,087.2 percent, revenues up 75.3 percent

Tong Ren Tang is a leading group of traditional Chinese medicine manufacturers. A trusted brand with a long history, it grows its own medicinal plants.

Chindex International, Inc.
NASDAQ: CHDX
Three-year trend: profits up 32.4 percent, revenues down 2.2 percent

United Family Hospitals Group, a division of Chindex, is one of the top foreign health care service providers in China—with facilities in five cities now open. It had 2006 revenues of over US$90 million, yet earnings and share prices have been relatively flat as the company has abandoned its products division and made heavy infrastructure investments, which may be a prelude to strong growth. Begun as a prime provider to the international community, one third of its patients are now Chinese.

Shinva Medical Instrument Co., Ltd.
SHA: 600587, A-shares
Three-year trend: profits US$2.67 million up from US$3.48 million loss,
revenues up 61.4 percent

Shinva makes surgical equipment in Shandong and sells to twenty-
one countries.

Jilin Leading Technology Development Co., Ltd.
SHE: 000669, A-shares
Three-year trend: profits up 555.6 percent, revenues up 6.53 percent

Jilin lists only three-hundred-plus employees but has posted steady
gains on its health care products.

Social Insecurity

Nothing is more important in the Chinese scheme of things
than longevity. Long life brings wisdom, respect, and blessings for
descendants—no shutting away of the old folks here. Get aged
enough and you might end up with a post in the Chinese government,
as an old joke goes. China is the only country where birthdays are cel-
ebrated not with cake but a healthy treat called Long-Life Noodles.
But if China is going to have a long-life health care system, who is
going to pay for it?

Since the start of the millennium, medical costs in China have been
increasing at an annual rate of 24 percent. Totaling over US$38.5
billion in 2005, that's quite a tab. And individuals now shoulder
60 percent. So in 2006 China issued a Health Insurance Regulation
Act—encouraging insurance firms to work with medical providers.
Back in 1997, the government had established a basic health scheme
for urban workers that led to 34.1 percent of urban workers being
covered by their employers. Still, 10 percent of China's population—
government officials, state enterprise workers, and some privileged

urbanites—have, until very recently, used up 98 percent of public health insurance funds. In the first quarter of 2006, health insurance fees were over US$3 billion, up 23.78 percent from the previous year.

Especially in a society with a growing population older than sixty (130 million in 2006), those families who aren't covered have begun to recognize the necessity of private health insurance. While most life and asset insurers offer some kind of medical coverage, insurance regulators only recently ratified five companies to start up as health-only underwriters. One of these got under way in 2005 with the claim of being China's very first health insurance company—appropriately, or predictably, named China People's Health Insurance Company Limited. Even more predictably, majority shares are held by China Life, once a state monopoly and still China's dominant insurance issuer. The health-only policy issuer isn't listed yet, but DKV, a German firm that is Europe's leading health insurer, has a 19 percent stake.

In late 2006, Chindex International (see above) also announced the first full-coverage PPO (preferred provider organization) scheme for Chinese nationals. This will pay for care at its own chain of hospitals as well as for care of ailments and accidents incurred worldwide. FESCO IB, the insurance division of China's Foreign Enterprise Service Corporation (FESCO), will share in the marketing and spoils.

By all logic, this should become a growing niche, with a general insurance industry that is measured as the fastest growing on the planet. (Are you surprised?) Growth averaged 30 percent from 1996 to 2004, bringing China's overall world ranking to eighth. The Chinese market is expected to exceed US$100 billion by 2008—though a country like Japan still spends four times more percentage of GDP on insurance costs. Life insurance policies account for three quarters of sales in China (though only an annual US$35 per capita). Such policies offer more lucrative payouts than banks do and also trade on the country's diminishing sense of personal security.

China Life was the only place to turn until domestic rivals were allowed to form in the early 1990s. Until the WTO agreement in 2001, foreign insurers were quite limited, but were allowed to make a gradual penetration for the next five years. By January 2005, there were twenty foreign life insurance firms in China, almost all joint ventures. And more are coming, increasing foreign market share from 2.6 percent to 12.7 percent already. But under the WTO, this industry, unlike the banking industry, has not been thrown wide open, only halfway. And locals China Life, Ping An, and Pacific Life held 70 percent of the market in 2005 and continue to lead because they receive more streamlined approval of the operating licenses required for separate provinces.

Still, the top policyholder continues to be the government, which collected US$105 billion in pension contributions, medical premiums, and other premiums. With a public till so large, hands have been dipping into social security funds. Various scandals erupted over 2006, with US$4 billion in funds "misused" in "overseas investments and unauthorized lending." No wonder the public wants insurance.

Jim's Sino Files: Insuring China's Future

Ping An Insurance (Group) Company of China, Ltd.
SHA: 601318, A-shares; HKG: 2318, H-shares; OTC: PIAIF
Three-year trend: profits up 154.3 percent, revenues up 39.2 percent

Ping An, based in Shenzhen, quietly holds 35 percent of the insurance market, extended to numerous subsidiaries that deal with corporate insurance and asset management. It has recently become the first insurance company to buy controlling interest in a fund management company and has teamed with China Life to purchase 10 percent of expanding Minsheng Bank as insurers look to diversify.

Generali China Life Insurance Company Limited (part of Assicurazioni Generali, BIT Italian Exchange: GASI) was the first joint-venture insurer (an unusual partnership between the Italian giant Generali and China National Petroleum) approved after China entered the WTO. It recently won a contract to back a massive US$2.4 billion pension plan.

At this writing, China Re is one of numerous insurance companies restructuring in preparation for a domestic IPO. While it is going to face more competition from foreign interlopers like Lloyd's, this government-controlled reinsurer holds a very dominant position within its specialized area.

PICC Property & Casualty Co., Ltd.
HKG: 2328, H-shares
Three-year trend: profits up 1,453.7 percent, revenues up 15.1 percent

PICC is a leader in the "non-life" field, though health and accident policies are represented. Despite recent jumps in profit, share prices have held back.

Insuring China's Future

From time immemorial, Chinese have sought to secure their children's future through education. No culture puts greater value on learning. Scholars, poets, writers, and thinkers, not warriors, were the most honored and privileged classes throughout the dynasties. Few statues of mounted horsemen can be found in China. But stone tablets in tribute to outstanding examination scores are common in many ancient sites. Unfortunately, there are still numerous suicides today when students fail the all-important National University Admissions Test.

While the government still takes on most education responsibilities, all the way through dozens of prestigious colleges, there's been a boom in all sorts of private schooling and preparatory help. In fact, it's proved a lucrative business, with supply hardly keeping up with newly prosperous parents willing to spend up to US$3,000 per year to give their products of the one-child policy the best leg up. Profit margins of private schools are estimated at as high as 50 percent, in part because teacher salaries are so low.

There are barriers and concerns over the legal status of private education: some diplomas aren't honored by the government, and the right for niche schools to earn reasonable returns was just asserted in 2005. And foreign input isn't quite welcome yet in state schools, where every textbook is politically sensitive. The government's main focus is bringing rural education up to par and waiving tuition for

150 million poorer children. Nonetheless, by the end of 2005, 15 million Chinese were attending some seventy-seven thousand private schools that seem pretty much off the radar. That accounts for 8 percent of children between five and fourteen and is sure to increase.

One example of this boom is in an area of critical importance to China—its food. Not many years back, the ancient secrets of culinary mastery were the exclusive domain of a handful of hidebound state-run institutes. Today, there are an uncountable number of cooking schools all across urban China, many run as adjuncts to restaurant chains, some encouraging women to try to take their place in the man's world of flaming woks.

That's just a start. Tutoring services; language, music, and even gymnastics schools; computer software; publishers of textbooks and other educational materials; specialized technical schools or those serving various religions; playground gear; chalkboards and lockers. Even uniform makers are going to benefit. Instruments for the school band, too, though they are pipas and erhus instead of tubas. China has even shown that it has the capabilities to attract others from the region to their classrooms: fifty thousand students from South Korea alone now study in China. Think of your own high school and alma mater and imagine all the companies that went into running a campus (and enabling you to cram for an exam all night in the library).

Remarkably, the enterprise of helping the country's next generations meet the grade is as yet barely reflected in the markets or listed stocks. Keep your pencils sharpened. China itself is like one big multiple-choice quiz where the questions and subjects change by the minute.

Jim's Sino Files: Some Homework

New Oriental Education & Tech. Group Inc.
NYSE: EDU, ADR
Three-year trend: profits down 10.8 percent, revenues up 58.5 percent

New Oriental helps privately prep Chinese for admission tests to foreign universities, emphasizing English. It is also developing materials and software and is targeting a million enrollees. Like other smaller competitors, this company is seeking to fill gaps in the state-run education system. With 3 percent of a fragmented market as of 2006, the company has been gaining brand recognition. Singapore's Raffles Education Corp. (SIN:5ES, S-shares) has bought 20 percent interest—and saw its share price shoot up 100 percent in 2005 due to its Chinese involvement.

Oriental Century Ltd.

SIN: 5II, S-shares

Three-year trend: profits up 41.7 percent, revnues up 61.3 percent

Similar-sounding Oriental Century sets up its own private schools, boarding schools, and kindergartens—plus a college under the name Oriental Pearl.

China Education Ltd.

ASX: CEH

Three-year trend: profits US$140,000 up from US$405,000 loss, revenues up 395.4 percent

Formerly EasyCall International, China Education runs a business college in northern Tianjin with 5,900 students and works with allied institutions and a number of subsidiaries involved in technical and computing courses.

Leadership for Life Inc., with both schools and Internet courses, will have an IPO soon. Its founder and CEO, Cindy Xi, was born in 1974.

Shelter from the Storm

For anyone seeing China when I first did, nothing could have been more obvious than the fact that housing was the country's number one bane and number one need. In big cities, most people lived in dilapidated projects or antiquated alleys or seized homes subdivided out of all utility. To be Chinese, it seemed, was to utterly lack personal space. People didn't just share apartments, they shared sides of a bed, with dozens using one kitchen tap and hundreds suffering at communal toilets that sent their characteristic odor across Chinese towns. Nobody had to pay rent, it was true, but the flip side was that there was little worth paying rent on (and no appreciation in forty years).

All that began to change slowly in the late eighties but didn't really take on full momentum until a massive privatization of state-held properties in 1998. Through the nineties, per capita spending on housing rose from under 1 percent to 5.6 percent. A vast exodus to newly built apartments, followed by the start-up of more upscale developments, has continued ever since. And the construction boom continues, with Chinese cities today littered with fanciful signs around gritty construction sites promising prospective condo owners the good life, with incongruous references to the Louvre, Picasso, the Riviera, and the Beatles. Huge fortunes were and are being made: of the one hundred richest men in China today, around half got that way thanks to real estate.

Can foreign investors do the same? On the one hand, China has huge pent-up demand that will take decades, maybe centuries, to satisfy. Even as recently as 2003, surveys indicated that 70 percent of the populace in China's prosperous coastal cities still weren't able to afford to purchase housing. On the other hand, today's property-development industry is probably the sector of the Chinese economy most rife with fraud and scandal. It's not uncommon for buyers to end up with less land and fewer amenities than advertised, or even holding the bag on previously mortgaged leases. Developers are renowned, too, for blithely ignoring codes and regulations mandating green space and facilities.

However, big and trusted names in land holding and construction, mostly from Hong Kong, are increasingly dominating, and professionalizing, the provision of new apartments and condos in the capitalist manner. Where for many decades China was rife with campaigns aimed against "landlords" and their inherited feudal privileges, the right to own property—and deal in it—has now been reestablished and reaffirmed in a long-awaited property law that will take effect in October 2007. It's important to note, though, that this new measure was passed more to reassure farmers trying to defend their turf from speculators than to encourage more housing starts.

Also, because of a scarcity of luxury property for foreigners, and the widespread use of real estate for speculation during long periods when the stock market itself was not yet trusted, China has already seen a rise in values comparable to those throughout the world during the recent period of global expansion and population pressure. There is hardly any difference at the moment between square-footage prices in Beijing and in Tokyo, despite the huge gap in cost of living. In other words, nobody is getting in on the ground floor any longer—whether as investors or in terms of owning property in China oneself.

Currently, real estate in China still isn't quite all the way real. Foreigners are technically allowed to buy only one property (though some have been discreetly purchasing one in each of various locales). And what anybody "owns" in China is just a lease to use the property for seventy years. While the government isn't ever likely to call in these chips, that theory has yet to be tested, and probably won't be until 2065. It's even less clear whether land will be freely traded on the open market.

If anything, the Chinese government has aimed all the policy weapons at its disposal toward slowing a hot property market—rising around 6 percent each year for the past four years—fearing inflation and an accrual of bad mortgages, as well as the social upheaval caused by prices out of most first-time buyers' range. (The average price of a 120-square-meter apartment in Beijing is US$110,000, while the average annual salary is only around US$6,000.) Through 2006 and 2007, a series of new measures have set penalties for speculation, tax evasion, price manipulation, and more. For instance, foreigners who hold property less than five years will now be taxed an additional 20 percent on all profits. Other laws on the books, not necessarily well enforced, set a limit on average size, in order to make apartments more affordable, and an added tax on developers' profits.

If there is one area that seems most likely to be headed for a hard landing, real estate would be it. Investment by developers continues to explode—up 21 percent in 2006. And prices in places like Beijing and Shanghai moved up by similar levels, even as unsold space and vacancies rose even more. While Chinese cities will take a long time to get overbuilt, they are clearly already overpriced. There could be sudden declines in value, and the Chinese government would cheer. And coal miners out west would hardly notice what happens to some condo dwellers in Shanghai. The economy as a whole might not even hiccup.

Still, many foreigners and overseas Chinese want to own their own place or a piece of the Chinese real estate action. If you are one of those foreigners or overseas Chinese who must have your own piece of the Chinese action, one smart move would be to look beyond the top-tier cities, where expatriates have formed their dollar-priced colonies. China has 128 cities with populations exceeding a million people, cities you've never even heard of. Jobs and industries are all moving westward, and there are many less developed inland locales that are underpriced and rife for expansion. Along the coast, places like Qingdao—a clean and prosperous port city that still bears the influence of having been a German protectorate—or any of the cities of Fujian—poised to link with a friendlier Taiwan—offer lots more upside to their lots with a sea view.

Residential housing, as huge a need as it is, is but one enterprise as China continues to rebuild from the ground up. Among the other monuments to modernity most worthy of potential investment, China will be upgrading and upsizing the American concept of the mall— and probably mall rats, too—in the years to come. From 2002 to 2003, the number of large shopping centers in China rose from three hundred to four hundred. Now it may be well over five hundred. Even smaller provincial cities are catching "mall mania." High-ticket items like big malls are sometimes rife with risk, as officials involved in land deals pressure local banks to finance where there may not yet be enough spending power. By the end of 2003, construction expenses for malls in China were estimated to top US$24 billion.

Heading all of this is Beijing's Golden Resources Shopping Mall, which weighs in with nearly 6 million square feet of shopping—and 230 escalators. Minnesota's famed Mall of America, in comparison, is a mere 4.2 million square feet. Said a spokesman for Golden Resources's developer, the unlisted New Yansha Group, at its opening back in October 2004, "We are the world's largest nation. The world's largest mall shows our progress as a society."

Already, however, it's been topped: Dongguan's South China Mall is half a million square feet more, featuring seven separately themed zones that are mini-cities modeled after Rome, Venice, and the Caribbean.

Jim's Sino Files: Constructive Criticism

Kerry Properties Ltd.
HKG: 0683, H-shares
Three-year trend: profits up 103.8 percent, revenues up 99.8 percent

Chinese exchanges are loaded with a glut of developers: picking one may be tougher than choosing an apartment. Kerry hardly sounds like a Chinese company, but it has been involved in some of the classiest projects in Hong Kong and on the mainland.

China Overseas Land & Investment
HKG: 0688, H-shares
Three-year trend: profits up 100.8 percent, revenues up 26.5 percent

Chinese nationals founded this company by investing first in Hong Kong and then securing licenses for projects back home.

Shui On Land Ltd.
HKG: 272, H-shares
Three-year trend: profits up 47.8 percent, revenues up 355.6 percent

A mega-force in Hong Kong, Shui On developed the acclaimed multi-use New World Shanghai, one of the modern city's must-see stops.

China Vanke Co., Ltd.

SHE: 000002, A-shares; 20002, B-shares

Three-year trend: profits up 145.4 percent, revenues up 132.8 percent

Founded in 1988, China Vanke is a less well known name with massive operations concentrated on residential housing and management in some of China's most prosperous areas, like the Pearl River Delta.

Sino Land Company Ltd.

HKG: 0083, H-shares; OTC: SNLAY, ADR

Three-year trend: profits up 327.3 percent, revenues up 96.9 percent

Another major developer of residential and industrial properties, as well as an investor in hotels and nightclubs.

China Fiberglass Co., Ltd.

SHA: 600176, A-shares

Three-year trend: profits up 48.1 percent, revenues up 76 percent

As its name suggests, this is the largest Chinese producer of fiberglass materials used for insulation. Less than 20 percent of Chinese homes have proper insulation.

CapitaLand Retail Ltd.

SIN: C31; OTC: CLLDY, CLLDF, ADR

Three-year trend: profits up 177.1 percent, revenues down 1 percent

CapitaLand opened its flagship shopping mall, Raffles City Shanghai mall, next to People's Square, right in the heart of the business capital. The company operates in twenty countries, including the Middle East. Through subsidiaries, it now has twenty-five shopping malls in China. It's one of those major hidden players in real estate development.

Hopewell Holdings Ltd.
HGK: 0054, H-shares
Three-year trend: profits up 47.5 percent, revenues up 42.6 percent

Hong Kong–based Hopewell has marked up 20 percent profit rises by keeping its fingers in everything surrounding the exploding and prosperous Pearl River Delta: property, hotels, convention centers, and retail.

Since most investors don't want to mess with tenants, taxes, or questionable titles, the better path may be to look at the most scrupulous developers as China's burgeoning middle class continues to seek better shelter and their own chunk of the Chinese dream.

9

Emerging China: The People's Republic of Tomorrow

Our tour around the formative frenzy that is China has traveled through some of the more intriguing corners of enterprise. By now, I hope it's inspired you to get out your charts and start exploring other regions of this vast country's even more enormous growth. Better yet, look around your own house, neighborhood, or familiar activities for the products and services that the Chinese may soon be needing.

No one book, not even a modern *Book of Changes*—or Yi Jing, China's classic Taoist text—could take in every aspect of the transformations to come. On this Chinese version of the board game Monopoly, Park Place and Marvin Gardens are still changing places. It's not a roll of the dice, but a corner on the best information, that will help you pass Go.

So here's my quick survey of other promising sectors to track, and possibly to plunk your money down on someday. I've also included my current views on currency, one of the main means of investing in China beyond the stock market. In this rapid rundown of enterprises nearly as new as China is old, each has a shot at carving out big earnings while helping define a modern China moving beyond its wildest dreams.

HIGH-TECH: As I write, two headlines from the daily overload of business briefs scream out at me. Both show how quickly China's high-tech sector is moving and how much the Chinese and American economies are being integrated. First, the White House Council on Environmental Quality gives a prize to Chinese PC-maker Lenovo for supplying U.S. federal agencies with "green" computers offering energy-saving innovations and recyclable packaging. Next, the Chinese government is said to have offered US$1 billion in incentives for Intel to open a large new chip plant in the northern city of Dalian.

China's day in the digital sun has arrived. Chinese laptops, made entirely with Chinese components, are already competing at lower cost with the world market's top end. Domestic computer sales, pushed by the upgrading of small-to-medium enterprises, hit US$15 billion by 2005 — the same year China passed the United States as the number one supplier of information technology (IT) goods, large or small.

Chinese companies haven't exactly done it alone: between 1999 and 2005, one hundred of the Fortune Global 500 companies — like Hewlett-Packard, Toshiba, and Samsung — set up research centers in China, among some 750 foreign-invested labs in the country. WTO membership and the relaxing of some barriers have also brought more of Taiwan's expertise and capital to this crucial area. Learning fast, Lenovo, for instance, pours US$300 million each year into technical innovation.

Now Chinese premier Wen Jiabao has urged the country to combat intellectual property theft in the best possible way — by creating more scientific patents and intellectual property of its own. Building on some promising Chinese work on genome mapping and robot design, artificial eyeballs, and superservers, official pronouncements say the next five years are crucial for the advances of Chinese IT, bioengineering, and manufacturing technology.

Companies: Surprisingly, the biggest player in China is Shenzhen-based Huawei Technologies, with centers in Bangalore, Silicon Valley, Moscow, etc., and with sales of US$8.2 billion for 2005. Allied with 3Com, Huawei Technologies provides wireless products, software, and technology to ninety countries, and sold 1.5 million notebook computers in 2006. Oddly enough, it has yet to have a stock offering; maybe it is doing well enough without one. Of course, **Lenovo Group Ltd. (HKG: 0992, H-shares; OTC: LNVGY, ADR; profits down 78.7 percent, revenues up 346.8 percent)** isn't just the IBM of China; it is IBM—and caters to 160 countries. Year 2006 revenues reached US$1.3 billion, making Lenovo big and dependable, but with big costs, too, and relatively low profit margins or stock price spikes. Lesser-known **Digital China Holdings Ltd. (HKG: 0861, H-shares; OTC: DCHIF; profits up 836.9 percent, revenues up 39.1 percent)** has partnerships with Cisco and is the largest distributor of IT products in China. **Beijing Teamsun Technology Co., Ltd. (SHA: 600410, A-shares; profits up 70.7 percent, revenues up 88.1 percent)** boasts similar results, but is much smaller, building its strategy, like the others, on the increased links among telecommunications, data storage, and computer simulation.

As in the rest of the world, there are fortunes to be made from this rapidly changing field—for those who have a clear picture of which areas are really ahead of others. When pursuing technology companies, my philosophy is to do even more homework than usual.

AEROSPACE: Never mind about China's Lunar New Year. One of these days in the not too distant future, Mother Earth just may find a Chinese face waving back at it from the lunar surface. The country's top secret rocket program originally began in 1956 (to keep up with the Russians). The Orwellian-sounding 5th Research Institute of China Aerospace Technology Group dominates satellite research. Now China's Chang'e program, named for a mythical spirit said to have traveled to the moon by imbibing a mysterious potion, is aiming to get there before 2017 by more conventional means—first as the world's fourth country to get a probe into lunar orbit, later with unmanned rovers, and then, who knows? While unconfirmed by research, the Chinese have hopes that minerals charged by the moon's constant solar barrage may someday help power mankind (especially the one fourth from China). On more solid ground, the government's current Five-Year Plan pledges to fund five to eight times the previous decade's number of satellites.

Companies: Shanghai Aerospace Automobile Electromechanical Co., Ltd. (SHA: 600151, A-shares; profits up 7.8 percent, revenues up 70.6 percent) straddles military and civilian work and makes everything from satellite-data-receiving equipment to auto parts to solar battery panels (its subsidiary Shanghai Solar Power Tech. Ltd. has a dominant market position). **China Spacesat Co., Ltd. (SHA: 600118, A-shares; profits up 1,541.3 percent, revenues up 160.6 percent)** rocketed on increased orders of smaller satellites. **Long March Launch Vehicle Technology Co., Ltd. (SHA: 600879, A-shares; profits up 53.8 percent, revenues up 70.6 percent)** sounds downright scary, and maybe it is — moving to develop weapons along with rocket guidance and satellite censors.

INTERNET: Will China change the World Wide Web, or will the World Wide Web change China? Nothing is exploding faster in an already explosive country. As mentioned previously, there were 137 million Net users in China at the end of 2006. This was an increase of 23.4 percent but still represents only 10 percent of China. So there's big room for a wide expansion of broadband. Amazingly, 76 percent of Chinese Net users had high-speed connections to more than 843,000 websites in Chinese, a jump of 150,000 in a single year. Web media — advertisements, games, downloads — grew 48 percent in 2005, 41.3 percent in 2006. Over eighty million Chinese bloggers are widening the parameters of free discussion, too. Some suggest that the products of a one-child policy are seeking company and connectivity with a vengeance. Unfiltered news and information, and a far wider range of entertainment choices than on stodgy state-run TV, are also helping send an entire generation to their terminals. Will it also send them to the barricades?

Companies: With far greater potential earnings, China's Internet stocks may be generally cheaper when compared to those in the United States. Despite government campaigns against teen addiction to online gaming, a growing social problem, **Shanda Interactive Entertainment Ltd. (NASDAQ: SNDA, ADR; profits down 13.1 percent, revenues up 27.4 percent)** claims 2.29 million active accounts. (This is not an endorsement of gambling stocks, merely more information for those who wish to pursue it.) QQ, an online community provided by **Tencent Holdings Ltd. (HKG: 700, H-shares; profits up 141 percent, revenues up 144 percent)**, claimed 580 million users at the end of 2006, 84.4 percent of China's instant-messaging market. **NetEase.com, Inc. (NASDAQ: NTES, ADR; profits up 181.6 percent, revenues up 139.6 percent)** is a slickly run online portal and community provider that has seen net profits jump 60 percent yearly.

FILM: Coming soon to a theater near you, Oscar winners made in China! China has a vibrant tradition of filmmaking stretching back to *Capturing Jun Mountain* at the turn of the twentieth century, through a golden age of vampish starlets in the 1930s, to the so-called fifth generation of film school grads like Zhang Yimou and Chen Kaige who broke from dreary propaganda with an infusion of realism and personal style.

But the slow conversion of fifteen state-supervised film studios and an invasion of U.S. products and fake DVD's left the industry reeling. As recently as 2003, box office receipts in South Korea, twenty times smaller than China, were five times higher. Even at last count, there was one movie house for every 125,000 Chinese viewers, compared to one for just over 8,000 Americans. With most Chinese watching DVD's in cramped homes, the modern cineplex should have strong appeal. Chinese even like popcorn.

Now Chinese film is rebounding with a blockbuster strategy: in 2006, eight expensive extravaganzas accounted for 70 percent of film budgets. And lesser ones still benefit from import quotas and requirements that two thirds of screen time be given to Chinese productions. The turnaround took off thanks to *Hero* in 2003, the first of many martial arts epics to shatter box office records and correct misperceptions about China's low production values. Since then, returns have leaped 25 percent per year, and new deals have been struck with American, French, and even Taiwanese companies for coproductions. While independent works still get careful scrutiny from government script readers, big productions are green-lighted more easily. As political scrutiny loosens, China will also become more attractive as an inexpensive (and atmospheric) location for foreign productions as well.

PricewaterhouseCoopers estimates that the global entertainment industry will grow 10 percent a year through 2010. China will provide most of that. Watch for more *Hero*s, made with more extras at less cost than MGM ever imagined.

Companies: Warner Bros., the state-owned China Film Group, and the private Hengdian Group (both unlisted) have partnered to create Warner China Films, which will produce Chinese-language films. This could have an eventual impact on **Time Warner stock (NYSE: TWX; profits up 94.8 percent, revenues up 5.1 percent). China Star Entertainment Limited (HKG: 0326, H-shares; profits US$4.7 million up from US$38.9 million loss, revenues down 7.6 percent)** is a major force in Chinese-language film and television dramas, and also manages artists. Huayi Brothers is a privately held production company with recent successes; 35 percent is owned by Hong Kong tycoon Li Ka-shing's somewhat less boffo **TOM Group Ltd. (HKG: 2383, H-shares; profits down 86.2 percent, revenues up 12.1 percent).** Hong Kong's **Golden Harvest Entertainment Holding Ltd. (HKG: 1132, H-shares; profits up 150 percent)** seems to be the first credit as distributor on every film in Asia, at least every one where the hero wears pigtails and slices up crowds with kung fu.

SPORT: Play ball! Did you know China already has its own fledgling baseball league (the CBL), to go with more successful leagues for China's two most popular sports, basketball (CBA) and soccer (the CPSL began in 1994 while the CSL, or football Super League, came ten years later but has been made less super by match-fixing scandals). There may not be many ways to invest directly in this sector yet—except through Asia-wide Star Sports TV, a division of Murdoch's News Corp. (NYSE: NWS), and other Western entities profiting tremendously from huge Chinese viewership and merchandising tie-ins. But the Chinese, once devoted to scholarship only, are becoming the most sports-minded of nations. During my earlier visits, I found myself the only jogger bothering to work up a sweat in the morning—and often running circles around Chinese engaged in more sedentary tai chi exercises. Elite leisure sports like skiing or tennis were either unknown or frowned upon; billiards and badminton took less effort, and took up much less room.

Now the 2008 Olympics will speed up the overall commercialization and marketing of sports, along with upgrading infrastructure that has lagged behind Western standards. Shanghai recently opened the world's largest and most advanced tennis center, to train future champions as well as host the ATP Masters championships. And let's not forget China's national pastime, Ping-Pong! Yao Ming of the Houston Rockets won't be the last of China's sports superstars to gain global marketing reach. And the astounding growth of golf in China, as previously mentioned, will also contribute to the rapid expansion of personal gyms, sporting goods, and apparel—whether in manufacturing or retail. Chinese don't just sew the laces for Nike and Adidas sneakers—they are wearing them now.

Companies: Ambitious gymnast Li Ning, one of China's first and most renowned Olympic gold medalists, has forged China's most recognizable local brand of equipment and shoes under his name. **Li Ning Co. Ltd. (HKG: 2331, H-shares; profits up 139.8 percent, revenues up 69.3 percent)** has seen over 20 percent annual increases of share prices and has established its products across China with a market share just below that of Nike (and the company exports to the Middle East). Sponsor and supplier to China's previous Olympic teams, it was outbid by Adidas for the Beijing Games. So Li Ning managed to place its branded jogging suits on China's Olympic broadcasters instead. A local competitor as yet unlisted, Anta (China) Co., Ltd., was founded in Fujian province in 1991 and by 2006 had established four thousand outlets across China.

PLASTIC MONEY: After years of sluggish acceptance and a confusing glut of issuers, China is warming up to the credit card—if not to credit itself. Loads of promotional giveaways and interest-free options brought the number of cards in China to sixty million in 2006. Not bad for a country where only a handful of VIP's got them for international use before 2004. And, as I recall, the very act of whipping one out prior to that was an exercise in futility. As recently as 2002, only 2.7 percent of merchants accepted cards and only 3 percent of spending was with cards. With most transactions still done in cash, you could definitely leave home without them. Also, there is not as yet a reliable network for tracking credit history or for preventing fake cards and fraudulent use.

You won't hear many stories, as you do in America, of credit cards being issued to pet cats and dogs. Qualifications are a bit more stringent, and lots of China's consumers, qualified or no, don't want anything to do with buying on time. The country's culture of careful saving has somewhat offset the lure of convenience and status. And a high percentage of cards are either barely used or paid off before charges get tacked on. That's why McKinsey has forecast Chinese banks may not earn profits on their cards until 2009. But the same survey estimated that by 2013, these banks would be in the black by something like US$1.6 billion. With inefficient banking one of the major sectors to be thrown open to slicker foreign firms, competition for customers is just revving up, and cards are sure to be a part of bundled services to be offered.

Companies: **Xpress Group Ltd., formerly China Credit Holdings Ltd. (HKG: 0185, H-shares; profits US$13.1 million up from US$14.1 million loss, revenues down 20.7 percent)** provides a wide range of card products, though its share prices have been relatively flat. Not listed as yet, China Unionpay, founded in 2002 and headquartered in Shanghai, runs the national bank card information switch network, an electronic platform sponsored by the Chinese government. **China Merchants Bank Co., Ltd. (SHA: 600036, A-shares; HKG: 3968, H-shares; OTC: CIHHF, CIHKF; profits up 107.4 percent, revenues up 58.6 percent)**, founded in 1987 and based in Shenzhen, may be China's best-run commercial bank, and its credit card business claimed ten million users by early 2007. In fact, with a doubling of card lending in 2006, profits were reported up 81 percent. Its latest promotion: a Hello Kitty fan card.

MOBILE PHONES: There's no such hesitance about another piece of technology that fits in your hands. It's estimated that the number of subscribers to mobile phone services reached 440 million in 2006, or a third of the population, while another 48 million were expected to join in 2007. This firmly places China as the top dog for this form of telecommunications. Maybe this is just the perfect product for a group-oriented society that's always on the go. And Chinese don't just use them to talk or send text messages; they play games, read ads, and access websites, all more cheaply than on computers. And China's manufacturers and service providers have been exposed to foreign brands and competition from the start: the WTO isn't about to hang them up.

Companies: Formed out of state interests in 2000, **China Mobile Ltd. (HKG: 0941, H-shares; NYSE: CHL, ADR; profits up 58.3 percent, revenues up 53.6 percent)** is not likely to lose its signal. It is simply the world's largest cell phone operator, with three hundred million subscribers in 2006. Of all the stocks on the Chinese market, it has the largest value, and is highest also among telecoms in Asia, and the company's thirty-one subsidiaries have assets that are over US$5 billion. Number two, **China Unicom Ltd. (HKG: 0762, H-shares; NYSE: CHU, ADR; profits US$137,000 up from US$0, revenues up 19.2 percent)** took a large loss in 2006 due to bond repayments, but its business indicators remained strong.

CABLE TV: Another sight that astounds me every time I check into a Chinese hotel is how many channels of cable television are available in this supposedly suppressed and rigidly controlled realm. Maybe the BBC suddenly goes to black when there's an unflattering report about Tibet, but most of the time Portuguese, French, Arabic, and Swedish programming plays along unfettered. There were, at the end of 2006, 139 million cable users out of 368 million families who own TV sets—and big international players like STAR and HBO are selling their content, betting they are going to have a lot bigger ratings soon. But less than 2 percent had digital cable, and SARFT, the government-controlled regulator of all major cable networks, has committed to a complete changeover—with the digital market projected to be worth at least US$64 billion by 2015, where it was US$5.13 billion in 2005.

Companies: **Shanghai Oriental Pearl (Group) Co., Ltd. (SHA: 600832, A-shares; profits up 12.6 percent, revenues up 40.1 percent)**

owns 29 percent of Shanghai's cable provider, with four million customers, plus a TV tower and a convention center. **Beijing Gehua
CATV Network Co., Ltd. (SHA: 600037, A-shares; profits up 112.2
percent, revenues up 41.7 percent)** plans to digitize all cable in Beijing
by 2008, though some analysts say this is unrealistic. In any event, net
profits rose 62.18 percent for the fourth quarter of 2006. China Cable
and Communication, Inc. (OTC: CCCI) is China's fastest growing
cable TV company—and the first foreign operator in the field. Shenzhen Topway Video Communication Co., Ltd., also unlisted, was the
first cable company in China, and is earning from high-speed Internet
and video on-demand services.

PUBLISHING: There's an even more amazing media blitz in evidence
on every stroll through urban China. Newsstands, or often just table-
tops set up on popular corners, sag with the weight of so many newspapers and magazines. Bookstores are overloaded, too.

While China's press and publishing industry could hardly be
termed free, in the editorial sense, it has certainly been unleashed.
There is a lot of self-censorship in the Chinese media, no doubt, even
by foreign news-gathering firms that have entered into joint ventures
to create Chinese Internet sites (like the Financial Times or Reuters).
There are a few topics that are simply not allowed in China, and most
firms merely steer clear of them. At the same time, some Western bestsellers are still flagrantly translated without permission and distributed in "underground" editions.

Between 1993 and 2003, book publishing revenues quadrupled. In
2005, there were 572 official publishers putting out around 220,000
titles per year. Even as the General Administration of Press and Publication (GAPP) helps the government keep as tight a rein as possible
on printed matter, the profusion of black and gray printed matter
continues to grow—from journals to state-controlled newspapers,
blatant rip-offs of U.S. bestsellers, and a thousand local versions of
"how to get rich quick" advice. Even state-run publishers openly sell
licenses to register new books and periodicals—US$6,500 per book,
double per periodical, has been the going rate.

And no government screening has deterred hundreds of start-ups of Chinese lifestyle magazines, or slowed an increase in newspaper circulations and advertising revenues. If policies are liberalized, or if exhausted government censors simply cannot keep pace, look out for the Hearsts and the Luces, the magazine chain moguls who will make sure Chinese read more than the tea leaves.

Companies: Stocks in the publishing industry can be as hidden as their owners' politics. Xinhua Media (SHA: 600825, A-shares) is a leading player in the newspaper publishing industry in Shanghai, controlled by Jianfang Daily Group. (Its parent company has been **Hualian Supermarket Co., Ltd.; profits down 54.9 percent, revenues down 38.9 percent.**) The similarly named **Xinhua Finance Media Ltd. (NASDAQ: XFML, ADR; profits US$3.34 million up from US$1.25 million loss, revenues up 14,642.5 percent)** got off to a shaky start with its March 2007 American IPO. The company was founded by Ms. Fredy Bush, a Mormon divorcée who went to Asia over twenty years ago. Similarly, the *People's Daily,* China's leading newspaper, and publisher of many affiliated titles around the country, became **Huawen Media Investment Corp. (SHE: 000793, A-shares; profits down 22.4 percent, revenues up 71.2 percent)**, whose main businesses merged with Hainan Minsheng Gas Corp. The M Media Group, part of the unlisted Morningside Group, founded in 1986 by Hong Kong's Chan family, won licenses for the Chinese edition of *Forbes, Harvard Business Review,* and more.

RETAIL AND FASHION: We end our survey right where we started it, with that most contemporary of consumerist pursuits: shopping. China's wonderful world of retailing grew 12 to 13 percent in total value in 2006 and is projected to grow 14 percent in 2007. And sales across the board should reach US$963 billion by 2010. That is not a misprint.

I've already mentioned the mega-malls showcasing foreign and international brands. They've already come a long way from the days when the only choices were muslin coats in black or blue. The country that is known for turning out much of the world's blue jeans and milling many of its textiles is already building some formidable brands in the world of casual wear. Increasingly, they will also be featuring Chinese names in the world of haute couture—look for new homegrown designers to follow in popularizing traditional Mandarin looks in the manner of overseas Chinese fashionistas like Vivienne Tam, Vera Wang, and Shanghai Tang's David Tang.

And when it comes to food merchandising, China's growth has already added superlatives to the supermarket biz. Here's an astounding set of numbers worth pausing on for a moment: at the start of the nineties, there was but one retailer in China that qualified as a full-fledged supermarket. By 2003, there were sixty thousand, with US$71 billion in sales. Just a tiny increase. I remember how excited people used to invite me into their homes in 1984, unabashedly eager to show off some new household appliance they'd obtained. Now, with 90 percent of Chinese having some sort of refrigeration, that has spelled doom to the old habit of fresh food marketing every day.

Giant foreign players, with expertise in supply chain organization that few local companies could match, jumped in as soon as regulations allowed, with France's Carrefour opening more than 130 all-purpose warehouses. United States master of "main street," Wal-Mart, got off to a shaky start but has now caught up through two masterful moves: winning official goodwill by dropping its antiunion stance to accept a government-backed labor organization, and gobbling up already established chains as a means to grow quickly in scale and cost efficiency without encountering too much red tape. In early 2007, Wal-Mart instantly passed Carrefour in volume by growing to over one hundred new stores, with the US$1 billion gamble of acquiring Taiwanese Trust-Mart. British Tesco, too, has bought 50 percent of smaller Hymall, another Taiwanese company.

But China's homegrown retailers like Lianhua, mentioned at the outset of our survey, will continue to gain as roads and infrastructure continue to improve, allowing distribution networks and chain stores to reach even the most remote areas. Imagine the sales figures when every village in the Chinese hinterlands has one of Lianhua's "Quik" convenience stores. With 80 percent of modern-format supermarkets in eastern coastal cities, the Ministry of Commerce has hatched plans to get more mini-marts and hypermarkets into the boondocks.

Companies: Beijing-based department store operator **Parkson Re-**

tail Group Ltd. (HKG: 3368, H-shares; OTC: PKSGF; profits up 216.9 percent, revenues up 158.9 percent) has at last count 37 of its own department stores, while managing others across China—part of an earnings rise forecast of 93 percent in 2006. It's a subsidiary of Malaysia's **Lion Diversified Holdings Berhad (KUL [Kuala Lumpur exchange]: 2887; profits up 26.3 percent, revenues up 347.1 percent)**, which has used its China connection to show good gains. **GOME Electrical Appliances Holding Ltd. (HKG: 0493, H-shares; profits up 62.4 percent, revenues up 154.5 percent)**, China's biggest electronics chain, has purportedly made Wong Kwong Yu the richest man in the new China at age thirty-seven (estimated wealth: US$2.3 billion). He announced in 2007 that he was using U.S. backer Bear Stearns to create a US$500 million fund for investing in mid-tier retail companies across China that need capital and improved management.

A true homegrown phenom in fashion, Metersbonwe Group, as yet unlisted, is one of China's leading clothes brands, with 1,800 outlets across China. Manufacturing, design, and marketing are all done in-house. Other big retailers, concentrating on casual wear, include Hong Kong–based **Giordano International Ltd. (HKG: 0709, H-shares; profits down 47.8 percent, revenues up 9.2 percent)**, which has grown to 1,700 shops in thirty countries, including 728 in China at last count, and **Bossini International Holdings Ltd. (HKG: 0592, H-shares; profits down 11 percent, revenues up 21.3 percent)**, which, despite its Italian name, caters to Hong Kong and the mainland. Not surprisingly, the market for business suits has been growing in China by 8 percent a year. **Youngor Group Co., Ltd. (SHA: 600177, A-shares; profits up 35.3 percent, revenues up 41.4 percent)**, based in Ningbo, provides shirts as well.

Two major local names that may be appearing more on shopping carts are **Beijing Hualian Hypermarket Co., Ltd. (SHA: 600361, A-shares; profits up 28.8 percent, revenues up 26.1 percent)** and **Lianhua Supermarket Holdings Co., Ltd. (HKG: 0980, H-shares; profits up 9.7 percent, revenues up 51.5 percent)**, whose rapid expansion was mentioned previously. At the end of 2006, Lianhua had forty-six thousand employees. **The Shanghai Friendship Group Inc. Co. (SHA: 600827, A-shares; 900923, B-shares; profits up 69.2 percent,**

revenues up 51.8 percent) has been quietly plugging along and runs over three thousand stores in eastern China. Department store chains Intime and New World are preparing Hong Kong IPO's.

CURRENCY: A lot of people have already figured out that keeping holdings in the Chinese yuan, or renminbi ("people's money"), may be a nice, relatively safe way to hitch an upward ride on China's growth. With the RMB finally unhinged from its strict dollar peg since 2006, daily fluctuations of 0.5 percent are permitted, and most see an increase in those margins and a gradual rise of at least 4 percent a year for the foreseeable future. I've gone further. I think it's reasonable to expect a 300 to 500 percent rise against the debt-ridden U.S. dollar over the next twenty years.

Do the Chinese want a stable environment for the financial sector, or do they want to correct a world trade imbalance and their own overabundance of speculative foreign capital? Do they let their own reserves and their banking industry take a hit? Or do they give in to pressure—political and financial, from China's partners and China's people—and continue to build in favor of rising export costs and increasing citizens' global buying power? Knowing the Chinese, they will do their best to navigate toward some "middle way." It's doubtful the Chinese government will want to see any steep inclines or declines without taking action. But the spotlight of the Beijing Olympics will certainly motivate them to make their currency as convertible as possible.

It's also possible at some point that all the hundreds of billions of dollars being poured into China will be pulled back, as people cash in when full convertibility arrives, and that could hurt the value temporarily. Still, people who invested in the Japanese yen when Japan was just establishing its manufacturing got to enjoy a strengthening against the dollar for a few decades. Nobody can even remember when the yen wasn't considered rock solid. I'm pretty sure it will be the same with the Chinese yuan. It's going to be big. It will be as important a currency as China itself will be—perhaps even the world's standard-setter someday.

Companies: Renminbi denominated deposits or bonds are available through organizations such as Everbank.com, as well as many international banks.

COMMODITIES: See my book *Hot Commodities* or the Rogers International Commodity Index. And see the figures charting China's rising demand in metals, energy sources, and grains.

With that, I've come to the finish line of my latest jaunt across China. I've tried to lay out the terrain ahead as best as I can, to be an advance scout of sorts and hopefully keep a bit ahead of the pack. Writing a book about China these days can't help making someone feel like some modern-day version of Sisyphus—the Greek mythic figure consigned to repeatedly rolling his rock up the same hill. A whole management class, a whole corporate world, a whole national ethos and infrastructure, are coalescing at fast-forward speed. Once you get to the finish, you've just got to start all over again—and revise all the information that can't keep pace with the constant daily deals, mergers, listings, innovations, policy reforms, and earnings announcements. In a backhanded way, though, having to update quickly is just more trusted confirmation that the story is still at its beginning, still picking up steam.

China, I'm convinced, is not going to fizzle out or fade away. But now it's up to you to figure out the best course for your Chinese journey and the best way to stay involved for the long haul. I trust that I've been able to point the way to a path and a country laden with possibilities. Just as I did the first time I glimpsed Shanghai's bustling waterfront or the stirring turrets of the Great Wall, you just might be asking yourself, "What took me so long to get here?"

Appendix

Our immigrant forebears were once told the streets of America were paved with gems. Ironically, it was the Chinese who dubbed San Francisco "the Old Gold Mountain." Well, despite all the great prospects I've outlined, the streets of China aren't quite laden with treasure. Some of them aren't paved at all, or still display more litter than glitter. And it doesn't matter if you are in Shanghai or Sheboygan, Wisconsin, or in Silicon Valley or Beijing's Silk Alley. Making money is hard work. That's true even when you are trying to make money in hand work harder for you. Again, the companies in this book are *not* recommendations. They are possible starting points.

If I've reported to you a lot of rising trends and share prices, that should make you all the more wary about buying into something that's already risen. Due diligence is always required. And luck favors the prepared mind, as other pundits and I have observed.

Whether Chinese stocks are going to become a central or marginal part of your portfolio or savings strategy depends on your own finances and life situation. Perhaps you will want to stick with commodities in high demand by China, or international companies doing business there, as a form of indirect investment.

To help you down the road further, I've gathered in one place the best websites for Chinese listings, brokers, and China-related funds. These Internet resources will offer you the most current and reliable data. When it comes to the specific sectors or companies that seem most sound and compelling, your personal understanding, analysis, and experience will have to point the rest of the way. As I've said: you do your research, pick the companies you like, and buy them, or you sit home and watch movies.

After all, China won't wait.

All China Shares

China Stock Directory (gives all share classes): www.chinaeconomicreview.com

www.hkex.com.hk/csm/search.asp?LangCode=en&location=CompanySearch

Shanghai A-Shares

www.chinaknowledge.com/financial/shanghai-A-shares.aspx (by subscription) or www.sse.com/cn (click link)

Shanghai B-Shares (open to foreign investors)

For current listings: www.sse.com.cn/sseportal/en_us/ps/bshare/lccl.shtml

Hong Kong H-Shares

Main Board: www.hkex.com.hk/tradinfo/stockcode/eisdeqty.htm

GEM (Growth Enterprise Market): gem.ednews.hk/company/e_default.htm

SOE Index (Hang Seng China Enterprise Index): www.hsi.com.hk/family/hscei_e.html

Red Chips (Hang Seng China-Affiliated Corp. Index):
www.hsi.com.hk/family/hscci_e.html

NYSE, NASDAQ, and OTC

Chinese stocks traded in U.S. and Canada:
www.ChineseWorldNet.com

Chinese companies:
www.wstock.net/wstock/us_cn.htm

Singapore Exchange Limited (SGX) S-Shares

Main Board: www.sgx.com

Chinese companies on Singapore stock exchange (in Chinese and
English):
www.sgx.com/chinese/listed_companies/Listed_Market_Summary
.shtml

London Stock Exchange L-Shares

London Stock Exchange: www.londonstockexchange.com/en-gb/

China-Based Mutual Funds and ETF's in the United States

Bloomberg Mutual Fund Center—China:
www.bloomberg.com

www.bloomberg.com/apps/data?Sector=779&pid=invest_
mutualfunds&ListBy=YTD&Term=1&x=18&y=6

Bloomberg ETF Center (China-related under Asia/Pacific):
www.bloomberg.com/markets/etfs/index.html

JV (Joint-Venture) Fund Management Companies

Complete list provided by China Securities Regulatory Commission:
www.csrc.gov.cn (click on link)

Index

ABOUT THE AUTHOR

Born on October 19, 1942, JIM ROGERS had his first job at age five, picking up bottles at baseball games. After growing up in Demopolis, Alabama, he won a scholarship to Yale. Upon graduation, he attended Balliol College at Oxford where he earned his first Guinness record as coxswain of the crew. After a stint in the army, he began work on Wall Street. He co-founded the Quantum Fund, a global investment partnership. During the 1970s, the portfolio gained 4,200 percent, while the S&P rose less than 47 percent. Rogers then decided to retire—at age thirty-seven—but he did not remain idle.

Continuing to manage his own portfolio, Rogers served as a professor of finance at the Columbia University Graduate School of Business and as moderator of *The Dreyfus Roundtable* on WCBS and *The Profit Motive* on FNN. At the same time, he laid the groundwork for his lifelong dream, an around-the-world motorcycle trip: more than 100,000 miles across six continents, his second Guinness record. That journey became the subject of Rogers's first book, *Investment Biker* (1994).

Rogers's Millennium Adventure 1999–2001, his third Guinness record, took him and his wife through 116 countries, through half of the world's 30 civil wars, and over 152,000 miles. His second book, *Adventure Capitalist,* chronicled that incredible journey.

Now a contributor to Fox News and other news and print outlets, he has recently moved to Asia with his wife and daughter.

He can be reached at www.jimrogers.com.

ABOUT THE TYPE

This book was set in Sabon, a typeface designed by the well-known German typographer Jan Tschichold (1902–74). Sabon's design is based upon the original letterforms of Claude Garamond and was created specifically to be used for three sources: foundry type for hand composition, Linotype, and Monotype. Tschichold named his typeface for the famous Frankfurt typefounder Jacques Sabon, who died in 1580.